TOVE HUSSEIN

AFRICA'S SONG
OF KAREN BLIXEN

view to the Ngong Hills from the farm veranda

AFRICA'S SONG
OF KAREN BLIXEN

TOVE HUSSEIN

ISBN 9966-9628-0-8

first published 1998

Tove Hussein
PO Box 46513
Nairobi, Kenya

---

photo credits: Karen Blixen Arkivet, Det Kongelige Bibliotek, 1, 2, 4, 5, 7, 8, 9, 10, 11, 12, 13, 14, 15, 16, 18, 20, 34, 37, 39, 42, 46, 52, 64, 69 top, 72, 74, 75, 83, 89, 96

private owners, ii & iii, 6, 43, 47, 48, 53, 58, 59, 60, 61, 68, 69 bottom, 76, 77, 81, 82, 91, 92, 93, 94, 95, 97, 98

Sunday Nation, Nairobi, 24 August 1969, 26

Jorgen Jessen, 38

Peter Hill Beard, 78

Berlingske Tidenende, 9 October 1964, 80

letters: with kind permission of Magister Clara Selborn, 23, 25, 27, 28, 29, 30, 31, 32

---

drawings: Maia Geheb 33, 50, 57, 63, 67, 71

layout: Helen van Houten

graphics & colour separations: Kul Graphics, Nairobi

printed by: Majestic Printing Works, Nairobi

Contents

One

Introduction

If I know a song of Africa,—I thought,— of the Giraffe, and the African new moon lying on her back, of the ploughs in the fields, and the sweaty faces of the coffee-pickers, does Africa know a song of me? Would the air over the plain quiver with a colour that I had on, or the children invent a game in which my name was, or the full moon throw a shadow over the gravel of the drive that was like me, or would the eagles of Ngong look out for me?'[1]

This quote is one of the many beautiful passages in Karen Blixen's famous book *Out of Africa,* published in 1938, seven years

The wilderness is cleared and rubbish collected in heaps for burning, circa 1913.

'We grew coffee on my farm. The land was in itself a little too high for coffee, and it was hard work to keep it going; we were never rich on the farm. But a coffee-plantation is a thing that gets hold of you and does not let you go, and there is always something to do on it: you are generally just a little behind with your work.'[2]

after she left her beloved Africa. She needed to distance herself from the painful memories of Africa, caused by the loss of the farm and her English friend, Denys Finch Hatton, before she could write about her life there. She had to wait several years after her return to Denmark before she could open the boxes with all her belongings that she had packed and sent from the farm. They contained too many sad memories. Despite the big losses she suffered there, Karen Blixen felt that the years she spent in Africa were the best and happiest of her life—partly because Africa gave her an identity, but also because it was in Africa that she lived her real life.

Karen Blixen has said that everything she wrote in *Out of Africa* was the truth. Her brother, Thomas Dinesen, who stayed with her on the farm for several years, has confirmed this, but he also added that her descriptions of life in Africa were seen through coloured glass.

There is, however, no doubt that Karen Blixen knew a song of Africa. In *Out of Africa* and its sequel, *Shadows on the Grass*,

Karen Blixen with her brother, Thomas Dinesen, in Africa, in 1922.

Thomas Dinesen visited his sister twice while she lived in Africa—the first time from December 1920 until March 1923, to find out if it was possible for him to settle in Africa. The second time he accompanied his mother, Ingeborg Dinesen, and they arrived in Mombasa on 3 November 1924. Thomas Dinesen left the farm again on 5 March 1925, together with Karen Blixen, Ingeborg Dinesen and Farah, but disembarked in Aden with Farah, concluding his visit to Africa with a safari in Somalia. Karen Blixen and her mother continued on to Denmark.

published in 1960, you can listen to this song. That it was her own experiences she described can be discovered by reading *Letters from Africa 1914–1931*, published in 1978. This collection contains many of the letters written to her family in Denmark while she lived on the farm. The letters describe her day-to-day life and tell readers the truth about some of the happiest as well as the more disastrous times Karen Blixen experienced. In *Out of Africa,* she illustrates how much she felt at home by writing that when she woke up in the morning she thought: 'Here I am, where I ought to be.'[3]

Karen Blixen's friend Denys Finch Hatton, who died in a plane crash shortly before she left Africa, came to live on the farm around 1922. He enjoyed having a story told and encouraged her to write down the stories she invented while he was away on safari. Upon his return, she would entertain him with these stories in front of the open fire after dinner. She also composed her stories when she needed to remove her thoughts from the problems of the farm.

When Karen Blixen returned to Denmark in 1931, she went to live with her mother, Ingeborg Dinesen, in her childhood home, Rungstedlund, where she started to write in earnest. Africa was not the subject of her first book, *Seven Gothic Tales,* which was published in 1934. *Out of Africa* was her second.

When I read *Out of Africa* the first time, Karen Blixen's love for the country and the African people made a lasting impression on me. She wrote:

'As for me, from my first weeks in Africa, I had felt a great affection for the Natives. It was a strong feeling that embraced all ages and both sexes. The discovery of the dark races was to me a magnificent enlargement of all my world.'[4]

It was the fate of the Africans who lived on the farm that worried Karen Blixen most when she was forced to sell the farm. Some of them had lived on this land long before it was turned over to European developers, others had settled here with their families, because they were working on the farm. Most of these 'squatters', as they were called, had nowhere else to go. The effort she made on their behalf, to try to force the colonial government to find a place where they could all live together, shows how much their welfare meant to her. From the day she said goodbye to the farm and the Africans who lived there, they remained in her thoughts, and through them she stayed in contact with her life in Africa, until she died 31 years later.

Karen Blixen always took an interest in her employees, and when she was alone at the farm, she had time to get to know them better. She visited them in their homes, took part in their celebrations and played with their children, invited the women to her house for tea, and organized parties for them. Gradually, she came to regard many of them as her friends.

Very few of her European friends were still living in Kenya by the time she left. The brothers Galbraith and Berkeley Cole, Erik von Otter and Denys Finch Hatton had already rested their bones in the African soil; Lord Delamere died the same year. So it was the African friends with whom Karen Blixen kept in contact after her return to Denmark. In the beginning, she sent them money every year at Christmas through her Nairobi solicitor, W.C. Hunter. His task was to distribute the money, as instructed,

Some of Karen Blixen's domestic staff photographed by Thomas Dinesen in front of a grass hut on the farm, ca. 1922. Left to right: Kamande wa Gatura, Isa, Abdullahi Ahmed Weid, Hassan Ismail, Juma's daughter, Mannehawa (also called Mohuu) and Juma bin Mohamed.

'The introduction into my life of another race, essentially different from mine, in Africa became to me a mysterious expansion of my world. My own voice and song in life there had a second set to it, and grew fuller and richer in the duet.'[5]

amongst her former employees and report back to her what each of them had said. Later she was able to establish more direct correspondence with her former staff members, and occasionally a traveller would bring her a verbal message. The letters contained happy as well as sad news and occasionally a request for financial assistance. Karen Blixen always helped as well as she was able. Upon her death, five of the employees from the farm or their children received a generous sum of money, which she had left to them in her will.

When I arrived in Kenya in 1968, a visit to her farm increased my interest in Karen Blixen and her writing. It was much later, however, when I became a founding member of the Karen Blixen Museum and spent more time on the farm, that I began to hear Africa's song of Karen Blixen for the first time.

A suburb by the name of Karen has developed around the farm, but the farmhouse itself has remained almost unaltered since it was built in 1911. It has now been transformed into the Karen Blixen Museum, and since opening its doors to the public in

1985, thousands of visitors have come to see if Karen Blixen's Africa still exists. For them, the author's life is a verse in the song they have heard of Africa.

I discovered that there is another song about Karen Blixen that is even more important when I started to search for the people who had once worked for her. Many of them were long gone, naturally, but as I talked to their families and listened to their memories of Karen Blixen, I decided to try to discover if there is an answer to her own question, 'Does Africa know a song of me?'

Several of the Africans whose fathers and grandfathers once worked on the farm had heard of Karen Blixen's generosity, her friendliness and interest in their families, which continued until she died in 1962. They had been raised with stories revolving around 'Mrs. Karen', 'Baroness Blixen', 'Memsab Blixen', 'Lioness Blixen' or just 'Karen Blixen'. Her picture is still hanging in a hut, in a shop, and in modern homes belonging to these families and, I have been told, occasionally inspires the telling of a story, just as the French hand-painted screen once did on the farm.

There is, however, one note in the African song that does not harmonize with the others. It comes from a Kenyan author who never met Karen Blixen but claims to have discovered in her writing a racist attitude in the way she describes African people. Not one of the many people I interviewed, some of whom knew Karen Blixen personally, agreed with his opinion.

Karen Blixen with Sofe and Tumbo, in 1930.

'It was a joy to come home to Farah's little boy; he is the most enchanting thing you could imagine; he will be two on the 25 of September and must be at the culmination point of delightfulness, from which he will come to descend for the rest of his life. His chief interest in life is Ngomas, of which we have had a whole lot on the farm recently; he can dance Kikuyu and Wakamba and sing as well, also the banned Ngoma, which is said to be very indecent but I didn't imagine he can understand that. Tumbo is his ideal and enjoys this position.'[6]

Two

Karen Blixen

Karen Blixen was born at Rungstedlund in Denmark on 17 April 1885, the second of Ingeborg and Wilhelm Dinesen's five children.

In 1913, she accepted a proposal of marriage from her distant cousin, Baron Bror von Blixen Finecke, and together they planned to go to Java to manage a rubber plantation belonging to her uncle Aage Westenholz.

But fate, in the shape of their mutual uncle, Count Mogens Krag-Juel-Vind-Frijs, would have it otherwise. Uncle Mogens, who had just returned from East Africa, where he had been on a big-game hunting safari, told the young couple exciting tales of his adventures in Kenya. He was confident that anyone with a love of adventure and capital to invest in the future of that country could make a fortune there. He had no

SS Admiral, the ship on which Karen Blixen sailed to Africa in 1913. Shown here are the Smoking Salon, Promenade Deck and Cabin on the SS Admiral.

'On 2 December 1913, Karen Dinesen left Denmark and, accompanied by her mother and her youngest sister, Ellen, travelled down through Europe to Naples, from where the German-East African Line ship Admiral sailed a fortnight later. She parted from her family in Naples, and the first letter in the collection was written on board ship to her mother, five days before Karen Dinesen was met by her fiancé on the quay at Mombasa.'[7]

Karen and Bror Blixen on safari, in 1914.

'I have spent four weeks in the happy hunting grounds and have just emerged from the depths of the great open spaces, from the life of prehistoric times, today just as it was a thousand years ago, from meeting with the great beasts of prey, which enthrall one, which obsesses one so that one feels that lions are all that one lives for—strengthened by the air of the high mountain region, tanned by its sun, filled with its wild, free, magnificent beauty in heat-dazzling days, in great clear moonlit nights. I must humbly apologise to those hunters whose delight in the chase I failed to understand. There is nothing in the world to equal it.'[8]

Karen Blixen was a keen hunter during her first years in Africa, but later on, when she had to take over the management of the farm, she put away her rifle.

difficulty in persuading the young couple to take up the challenge, and Bror went ahead to purchase a cattle farm in Kenya. While he was staying at the Norfolk Hotel in Nairobi, he met and talked with several of the earlier settlers, who convinced him that coffee farming was more lucrative than dairy farming.

Karen Dinesen arrived in Kenya on 13 January 1914. The wedding took place the following day in Mombasa and, after a honeymoon safari to Uncle Mogens' hunting farm on the shores of Lake Naivasha, they settled into married life on Mbagathi, the farm Bror Blixen had bought, 20 kilometres outside Nairobi. Here they started planting

Karen and Bror Blixen on their way to a ngoma, in 1914.

'There was a surprise in store for me when we arrived at the farm. All the thousand boys were drawn up in ranks and after a really earsplitting welcome they closed ranks and came up to the house with us, surrounded us when we got out of the car and insisted on touching us,—and all those black heads right in front of one's gaze were quite overwhelming.'[9]

The picture was not taken on their arrival at the farm but shortly after, when they were on their way to a ngoma, held in honour of the visit of Prince Wilhelm of Sweden. They are here both dressed according to the latest fashion, as Karen Blixen liked to be well dressed on festive occasions and in the evenings. During the day, however, she was often dressed in old, worn-out and oil-stained khaki trousers and shirt.

coffee on 600 acres of the 4,500 on the farm. Mbagathi was owned by Karen Coffee Company, with Aage Westenholz as the main shareholder and chairman and the families of both Karen and Bror Blixen as investors. In 1917, Karen Coffee Company purchased the much bigger farm Mbogani, and the Blixens moved into their new beautiful farmhouse, which became Karen Blixen's home until she left Kenya.

Bror Blixen soon became bored with life as a farmer, and when the First World War broke out in 1914, he joined Lord Delamere's troops near the Tanzanian border. After the war, Bror was often away on hunting safaris, and in his absence, Karen

Bror Blixen in the office at Mbogani, circa 1917.

'I am sitting writing in Bror's smoking room or office,–at Frydenlund,– the only room that is in order so far.... We are very fond of this room; it has a ten-foot-wide window on to the veranda and is always beautifully cool and shaded; it is furnished with Sjögren's things and some of our own from Mbagathi, and it is a great advantage for Bror to have a peaceful room where he can write and keep his papers. There is only one door, as in the office at home, so there is no through passage, and only people who have something to do come in here.' [10]

Blixen, together with her managers, had to take an active part in the running of the farm. Eventually, the shareholders insisted that Bror should have nothing more to do with the management of the farm, and he moved out in 1921. The Blixens were separated in 1922 and later divorced.

In 1918, Karen Blixen met Denys Finch Hatton at the Muthaiga Club, in Nairobi. They soon became good friends, and Karen Blixen saw in him the intellect she found lacking in her own husband. When Bror Blixen moved away from the farm, Denys Finch Hatton brought his personal things to Mbogani and began to stay there between his safaris.

The coffee farm was not a success. The first coffee trees were planted when the war broke out, and bad luck followed in its footsteps. It was difficult to get workers during the war or even after it had ended. A combination of too little rain and coffee berry disease also did nothing to increase the harvest. The low coffee prices in 1922 were followed by a reasonably good year, but in 1924, there was again very little rain. During the next four years, coffee prices were on the increase, but then the grasshoppers came and ate everything in their way. It was becoming evident that many coffee farms were situated in areas where neither the climate nor the soil was suitable, and Karen Blixen's farm turned out to be in one of those areas. The Great Depression, which started in 1929, finally put an end to Karen Blixen's life as a coffee farmer, and she was forced to sell the farm in 1931.

It was not only the loss of the farm and the thought of her own insecure future that made Karen Blixen unhappy when she had to leave Africa; she also felt that she was abandoning all the Africans who lived and worked on her farm. They had become dependent on her, and they now trusted her to look after them.

'However it may have come about, it is clear to me by now that my black brother here in Africa has become the great passion of my life, and that this cannot be changed. Even Denys, although he makes me tremendously happy, carries no weight in comparison.' [11]

Bror Blixen plants the first coffee tree, in 1914.

'You plant a little over six hundred trees to the acre, and I had six hundred acres of land with coffee; my oxen dragged the cultivators up and down the fields, between the rows of trees, many thousand miles, patiently, awaiting coming bounties.' [12]

Karen Blixen on safari, in 1918.

visit the Africa she described so fascinatingly.

There were other women amongst the early pioneers who, like Karen Blixen, had a farm in Africa and who wrote a book about their unique adventures. Many of them lived very far from civilization; their farms were pieces of wilderness, and they often started life on their new farm living in a simple grass hut until the fields were cleared and planted, and time was spared to build a proper house. Everything had to be brought with them to the farm as, apart from the Indian duka by the railway station, there were no other places to find provisions. If someone on their farm got sick or hurt, they had to rely on themselves for medical care.

These authors also knew a song of Africa. But although their adventures make interesting and exciting reading, it is Karen Blixen's descriptions, her insight and understanding, and her great talent for writing that have led many to consider *Out of Africa* the best book ever written about the continent. She wrote with the hand of a true artist, which makes her works rank above those of many of her contemporaries.

There is no doubt that it was in Africa that Karen Blixen matured to write the stories that have made her into the world-famous author we know today. Her beautiful book about Africa has certainly made an impact on many people, not only in Africa, but in many other parts of the world. Since the publication of *Out of Africa,* her readers have been influenced to come to Kenya to

Three

A Farm in Africa 1914–1931

It was the railway that brought the first white settlers and Indian traders to the interior of Kenya. By 1901, it had reached Lake Victoria, five years after the first yards of rail had been laid in Mombasa. It put an end to many thousands of years of isolation, and it started a new era that was to change the future of the African people.

It is difficult to get a concrete answer as to why this 'lunatic railway', as it was nicknamed, was built. Some are of the opinion that it was built to connect Uganda with Mombasa, the seaport of Kenya. Others suggest that it was to open new and rich areas for settlement, or to end the slave trade. Yet another theory is that the railway was built for the sole purpose

Women and men, each with a jembe, are loosening the soil in the coffee field, circa 1913.

'Time seems to pass so quickly here.–it is interesting to watch the plantation and quite remarkable when I think that the thick dark forest, with a narrow little green path through it, that I was walking along on 15 January when I came out here with Bror, has turned into the smooth peaceful coffee field, which is kept in exactly the same orderly way as the kitchen garden at home.' [13]

of giving Britain control of the Upper Nile, thereby keeping a firm grip on Egypt and the Suez Canal. The result was, however, that it became possible for white people to colonize the country and cultivate the fertile interior highlands.

The railway cost the British taxpayers five and a half million pounds, and the only way to make it pay for itself was to develop the land on both sides of the 580-mile-long stretch, which ran mostly through uninhabited regions. An aggressive campaign in England resulted in the arrival of the first white settlers in Kenya, in 1903. These were real pioneers. No roads led to the farms they had purchased, which were usually just an expanse of forest, plain or bush. They had to decide for themselves whether to have cattle, sheep, potatoes or maize. There was no one to help with advice or information about the lurking dangers of unknown diseases, which could wipe out a herd or an entire crop. Agriculture was a gamble in the beginning, and many had to give up and leave their farms, having lost everything they had invested.

Bror Blixen arrived in Kenya in 1913, along with a steady stream of settlers from Scandinavia, England, Australia, Ireland, France, Scotland, America, and especially South Africa. They were enticed by the many

Women planting coffee trees, circa 1913.

'Coffee-growing is a long job. It does not all come out as you imagine, when, yourself young and hopeful, in the streaming rain, you carry the boxes of your shining young coffee-plants from the nurseries, and, with the whole number of farm-hands in the field, watch the plants set in the regular rows of holes in the wet ground where they are to grow, and then have them thickly shaded against the sun, with branches broken from the bush, since obscurity is the privilege of young things.' [14]

advantages offered in Kenya, which had a population of only three million, vast areas of cheap land, and a mild climate without winters. In addition, there was plenty of building material and a nearby railroad to transport any produce to the capital city, Nairobi, or via the port of Mombasa to Europe.

Several crops were tried during those first years, but coffee became the most important, especially on the land between the Kikuyu and the Maasai areas around Nairobi. It required an immense workforce to clear the African bush and to plant the fields. In the beginning, it was very difficult to obtain a sizeable workforce. Traditionally, it was the African women who tilled the soil. The men were warriors and took care of the tribe's internal politics. The settlers tried to persuade the local chiefs to send their young men to work, but as they were not used to the hard and regular labour and had no experience in the use of tools and machines, most of them soon disappeared again. A hut tax was introduced, which required each family to pay an annual tax amounting to an average farmworker's monthly salary. The money could be obtained

Young coffee trees, circa 1913.

'In the wilderness and irregularity of the country, a piece of land laid out and planted according to rule, looked very well. Later on, when I flew over Africa, and became familiar with the appearance of my farm from the air, I was filled with admiration for my coffee-plantation, that lay quite bright green in the grey-green land, and I realized how keenly the human mind yearns for geometrical figures. All the country around Nairobi, particularly to the north of the town, is laid out in a similar way, and here lives a people, who are constantly thinking and talking of planting, pruning or picking coffee, and who lie at night and meditate upon improvements to their coffee-factories.'[15]

by the sale of farm animals or crops, but as the Africans did not like to part with their animals, they often had no choice but to sell their labour.

When an African worker was employed by a white settler, he became a 'squatter'. This meant that he could move his family and livestock to a piece of the settler's uncultivated land where, according to the rules, the settler had to provide water and firewood, and look after the worker's general health. Although the colonial government had rules to prevent settlers from abusing their workers, there were cases in which workers were treated poorly or unjustly.

When Karen Blixen moved from the old Mbagathi farm to the much bigger neighbouring farm at Mbogani, in 1917, she not only moved into a fully furnished house but she also took over the responsibility of a village full of squatters who had already lived on her land for many years.

The African farm, Mbogani, bought in 1917.

'I had a farm in Africa, at the foot of the Ngong Hills. The Equator runs across these highlands, a hundred miles to the North, and the farm lay at an altitude of over six thousand feet. In the daytime you felt that you had got high up, near the sun, but the early mornings and evenings were limpid and restful, and the nights were cold.' [16]

This photograph of Mbogani was taken in 1917, when the Blixens moved here from the much smaller farm, Mbagathi. Karen Blixen is standing next to the entrance to the veranda on the east side of the house. The coffee fields are in the area behind the photographer. On the stone-paved terrace on the western side of the house, Karen Blixen often sat by her millstone table and enjoyed the view to the Ngong Hills.

During the years that followed, several more arrived.

Karen Blixen enjoyed visiting the families of her domestic staff and often passed by their houses when she was walking with her dogs. Her friendly manner and interest in the welfare of her squatters and workers was commonly known but far from accepted by other Europeans in the colony. Many of them gossiped about her and called her 'pro-native'. They were convinced that it would spoil the efficiency of the workers if she became too friendly towards them. Karen Blixen wrote about her staff:

'I had in Africa many servants, whom I shall always remember as part of my existence there. There was Ismael, my gun-bearer, a mighty hunter brought up and

Karen Blixen with eight Africans on the veranda in front of her house on the Mbogani farm, in 1917. Back row, left to right: Nganga, Abdullahi, Mohamed Noor and Njoroge Wachegi. Front row, left to right: Rashid bin Juma, Farah Aden, Said bin Bakar and a friend of Farah's who was visiting when the picture was taken.

Karen Blixen is here dressed all in white with a flower tucked into her belt. The long amber necklace she is wearing was a gift from Farah. Although most of the Africans who worked in the house were Somali, she also employed peaple from other tribes, for example, Kikuyu, Kavirondo and Wakamba.

trained exclusively in the hunter's world, a great tracker and weather prophet, expressing himself in hunter's terminology and speaking of my "big" and my "young" rifle. It was Ismael who after his return to Somaliland addressed his letter to me "Lioness Blixen" and began it: "Honourable Lioness". There was old Ismael, my cook and faithful companion on safaris, who was a kind of Mohammedan saint. And there was Kamante, a small figure to look at but great, even formidable, in his total isolation. But Farah was my servant by the grace of God.'[17]

In the years that followed, several other Africans came to work on the farm as domestic workers for shorter or longer periods. There was Farah's cousin Abdullahi, Juma bin Mohamed, Ali bin Hassan and Hassan Ismail, just to mention some of those best known through Karen Blixen's writings.

Every morning after breakfast when possible, Karen Blixen turned her veranda into a clinic. The farm workers could be treated there for minor cuts, bruises, burns or colds; but she also applied herself, with great enthusiasm, to treat cases like chicken pox, cholera, malaria, dysentery, broken bones, sprains, infections and influenza. Her workers had, of course, their own traditional remedies and often came to her only when those had failed, or out of curiosity, or to be entertained. They all hated to be sent to hospital. Workers even came from other farms for treatment.

Kamande's first visit to Karen Blixen's house was as a patient, and he eventually became her assistant nurse. Once Kamande made an almost fatal mistake by giving a patient the wrong medicine; however, this did little to damage the popularity of Karen Blixen or himself as gifted healers.

Karen Blixen always listened when her workers came to her with their problems, and she tried her best to help them settle their disputes. In difficult cases between the Kikuyus, she sometimes had to call Chief Kinanjui, the local chief of her Kikuyu workers.

She had a very good relationship with the many Somali workers who lived in a separate village on the farm. They were strict Muslims and had their own religious laws, which guided them in all domestic matters. Karen Blixen had to familiarize herself with their holy lawbook in order to try to mediate in their disagreements. If they could not settle them, they had to travel to Nairobi to consult a Somali judge or council. In time, Karen Blixen became very interested in their religion, Islam, and often discussed its principles with Farah.

Karen Blixen started a school on the farm when several of her employees wanted their children to learn to read and write. Europeans at that time were not in favour of educating Africans, and Karen Blixen met resistance from her farm manager, who was convinced that educated Africans would become troublesome workers. She managed eventually to convince him that the school would draw more workers to the farm, and with the blessings of Chief Kinanjui, Karen Blixen opened her school in 1924. The children were taught during the day, and adults who wanted to learn to read and write were encouraged to enroll in the evening classes.

She often lent money to her workers, and wrote to her brother, Thomas:

'you know, for instance, that in my relations with the natives, which mean so much

Karen Blixen's mother, Ingeborg Dinesen, with Chief Kinanjui at a ngoma on the farm, in January 1925.

'The Ngomas were held sometimes in the day and sometimes at night.' [18]

Karen Blixen liked the night ngomas best, because they took place by full moon with large bonfires on the lawn, and they gave the dance unity and effect. Chief Kinanjui was often present at the big ngomas and Karen Blixen described him thus:

'He was always an impressive figure, tall and broad, with no fat on him anywhere; his face too was proud, long and bony, with a slanting forehead like that of a Red Indian.' [19]

to me, it is almost impossible for me not to do things for them on a grand scale, far grander than my position really allows. Of course that is wrong. But it is what gives so much of my happiness here and so much meaning to my life. Of course it can be said that one can help them with other things besides money, and I think that I do that; I give up a great deal of my time to them, with my doctoring, for instance, and of my strength,—and yet here again it is money that represents the violinist's hands; he may well be just as great an artist without them, only God can know that, and who else has any joy of it? The natives have been so hard up this last year; the money that I have lent them here and there,—1,600 shillings,—I have not the heart to demand from them now.' [20]

During the seventeen years Karen Blixen lived in Kenya, she often wrote to her family in Denmark about her staff and their children. Kamande, who was later made famous by Karen Blixen in *Out of Africa,* is just one example of how her interest in him was to shape his life. Kamande was initially employed to look after Karen Blixen's dogs and later rose in the ranks to become her assistant nurse; but when she discovered that he had a special talent for cooking, which she described as an artform, he became her cook until she left the country.

In 1975, I went to visit Kamande for the first time. Later, he was a great help when the Karen Blixen Museum in Nairobi was being decorated. He not only remembered where the furniture had been placed, but he also helped distinguish the genuine furniture from the numerous pieces that were offered to the museum from households around Kenya, claiming to be 'original' Karen Blixen furniture.

Kamande once told me what he remembered about Karen Blixen:

'Mrs. Karen was like a mother to me. She was a good woman, and did not treat people differently. She liked everyone on the farm, no matter which tribe they belonged to, even the Mohammedans. People who came to the farm could not believe that it belonged to a mzungu, because we could graze our cows and sheep where we liked. People from other farms could also come to live on her farm. She would give them a piece of land, where they could grow crops and graze their animals. Mrs. Karen said that the land, the birds and the trees did not belong to her but to God. She would also sometimes protect people who had run away from other farms, if she thought that they had been badly treated. Once a week, she slaughtered a cow and divided the meat equally amongst us, or she rode out on the plain to shoot game to give us the meat. But she could also become very kali, and once she slapped me.' [21]

Karen Blixen knew most of the children who lived on her farm, especially those of her domestic staff. They brought their fathers' cows and goats to graze on the front lawn, and they played inside her house. She often took them on small excursions in her car to entertain them, and she talked about them in many of her letters home as her adopted children. Together, they walked to the dam to catch fish or crossed the river to look at the wild animals on the plain, and on Sundays, they came to her house to listen to her gramophone. Juma's children, the boy, Tumbo, and the girl, Mohuu, the little motherless Halima, Kamande's younger brother, Titi, and Farah's little boy, Sofe, were her favourite playmates.

'I had Juma's little girl with me,—Uncle Aage has seen her,—she has come to seem more and more like my adopted child and is quite mad about driving in the car.' [22]

'It is dreadful to have as many foster children as I have.' [23]

Mohuu and Tumbo were indulged with gifts, clothes and outings in the car. Tumbo was sent to boarding school in Pumwani, a suburb of Nairobi, and Abdullahi, Farah's cousin, was sent to a Muslim school in Mombasa. Karen Blixen arranged this and helped to pay the school fees. She had discovered in the two boys an intelligence that she felt ought to be developed. She wrote this about Tumbo:

'On my walks I always have Tumbo and Titi as my companions and to look after the dogs; they are exactly as two puppies themselves, rush about all over the place bubbling over with laughter over everything. Tumbo has grown into a real boy, with a catapult and "gruesome cries at night", he is a bright kid.' [24]

The keen interest Karen Blixen took in her employees was unusual for a white woman during the colonial days in Kenya; most of them spent little time with their staff, beyond what was necessary to give the daily instructions regarding the household. Even fewer took an active interest in the African children, their education and future. Karen Blixen was a remarkable woman in many ways, and she felt responsible for the physical as well as the mental well-being of her staff. Before she left the farm for good, she wrote to her mother:

'The great trust that all the black people place in me, and in my ability to arrange everything for the best for them, and my own awareness of the appalling insecure basis of it, use up all my mental powers, as it were.' [25]

When Karen Blixen left Africa, she had approximately 200 families living on the farm, and together they owned over 3,000 head of cattle. As the farm was to be sub-

Somali women knitting, with Fathima Barud in the middle, ca. 1930.

Karen Blixen spent many hours in the company of the Somali women on the farm and often stopped for a chat when she passed Farah's house on her evening walks. 'They took an interest in everything, and little things pleased them. Small mishaps on the farm, and jokes on our local affairs, set them laughing like a whole chime of jingles in the house. When I was to teach them to knit they laughed over it as over a comical puppet-show.' [26]

divided on her departure into building plots, they could no longer stay there. Most of them had nowhere to go; the government had no solution to the problem, and there were no laws to protect them. Karen Blixen spent the last months before she left visiting various land and government offices, in an attempt to extract promises of land for her workers and squatters from government officials, who had no land to give her. It was an enormous and exhausting task, which was not lessened by the squatter's own inability to decide amongst themselves where they wanted to settle. Finally, a piece of land was found in the Kikuyu Reserve where there was enough room for them all.

By this time, some of her house staff had made other plans for their future. Farah wanted to go to Somaliland, but he had several businesses in Kenya that had to be sorted out first. Abdullahi had had a disagreement with Farah and had already left the farm.

Juma wanted to be registered as a Maasai and settle in Maasailand with his mother's people. Karen Blixen not only helped him to do this, but she also helped him to get land and build a house. Ali wanted to learn to drive, so Karen Blixen taught him to drive in her own car and helped him to obtain a licence before she left. Everyone had to be remembered, helped and taken care of, and she also divided and distributed the cows, calves and geese amongst her staff and their children.

Kamande was her biggest worry, because she suspected that it would be difficult for him to find work, and therefore it was important for her to obtain land for him from the government. When she left, Karen Blixen gave his son Titi a small bull as a parting gift.

Today, there are few people left with direct connection to the farm, but their children and grandchildren still remember the stories told to them by their fathers and grandfathers about life on the farm.

In the following chapters, it is my aim to try to bring to life the song they know about Karen Blixen, about how she kept a line of communication open with their families long after she settled back in her native Denmark, and how she was always ready to help them until she died in 1962. And I want to illustrate the influence Karen Blixen had on the destinies of those families.

Four

Letters 1931–1962

When Karen Blixen returned to Denmark in 1931, she did not forget her African friends. She kept in contact with them through her Nairobi solicitor, W.C. Hunter & Co., who always knew where to contact Farah, who lived in the Nairobi suburb of Eastleigh when he was not away on safari or business.

To send money to her old staff at Christmas time, her solicitor had to contact Farah first, who then sent messages to all the others from the farm. In return, all Karen Blixen asked was for an update on their lives during the past year, as dictated to the solicitor's clerk. The clerk wrote down their news and relayed it to her. Some had difficulty expressing themselves in the luxurious law office and preferred to go to the post office where an Indian letter writer was seated outside at his little desk, in the shade of an eucalyptus tree, with his typewriter in front of him. For a small fee, it was much easier for them to compose a proper message in more familiar surroundings.

A letter from Juma carried the following news: 'Some fire came into my house and ended one excellent goat.'[27]

Ali Hassan wrote: 'Things was not very good here. If the old Memsahib was been in this place, this people would not behaved such as they do.'[28]

Fortunately, Karen Blixen had the imagination necessary to translate their cryptic messages. In her book *Shadows on the Grass* she imagined Kamande on his way to the post office, composing his thoughts in his head in his mother tongue, Kikuyu. In front of the Indian scribe's desk, he would have to translate his message into Kiswahili. Finally, the scribe would translate the letter into English—a language he himself had not fully mastered. Karen Blixen would have to search for the original message under many layers of translation.

One of Kamande's letters contained this happy news: 'I got newly female infant from my wife, who is somewhat good sort.'[29]

Karen Blixen was sure that Farah dictated his messages in English himself for, as she said: 'They were much like him, gravely and gracefully standing on his own dignity and mine, avoiding any manifestation of pity for any of us.'[30]

Farah's cousin Abdullahi had been to school and was perhaps the one best able to write letters, even if his letters, according to Karen Blixen, were not as substantial as Kamande's.

Karen Blixen wrote a letter to Abdullahi in 1936, telling him that she was writing a book about the farm and all the people she had known there. Abdullahi replied that he had commissioned three holy men to pray that the book would be a success, and that he hoped that it would earn her enough money to enable her to buy him a typewriter.

Dear Madam

With whole of my heart I send you happy Xmas and happy new Year – 1960

Best wishes and good for the coming years.

I still remember you for the years passed and I shall remember your for the coming years.

Yours faithfully,

ALI HASSAN.

Letter from Ali bin Hassan to Karen Blixen, in 1959.

Karen Blixen did send him a typewriter, which eventually reached him via train, ship and camelback. Abdullahi thanked her by writing a letter on it.

When World War II broke out, Karen Blixen lost contact with her African friends, but she writes about them in *Shadows on the Grass,* describing how they often came to her in her dreams. As soon as the war ended, Karen Blixen wrote to W.C. Hunter & Co., in Nairobi, to learn about them. She discovered the sad news that Farah had died, and therefore it was impossible to contact the others. A few months later, however, she was pleasantly surprised when she received a letter from the British governor in Kenya, Sir Philip Mitchell, explaining that he wrote on behalf of Ali Hassan, who now was working in his house. She was very happy to hear this and immediately wrote back.

In *Shadows on the Grass,* Karen Blixen relates what Ali had told Sir Philip:

'. . . he looked upon himself as still being in my service, and that if I ever came back to Africa he would feel free to leave Government House without notice. Here Ali at least had come forth, then, in great state, accompanied by the Lion and the Unicorn. He would order the others back as well, and we would all be gathered together once more.'[31]

Karen Blixen continued to correspond with Ali, whose letters, amongst other things, told her that Juma had become an old man with grandchildren and that his son Tumbo was a lorry driver in Nairobi. Sofe, Farah's son, then 17, was supporting himself successfully as a horse trader and was about to marry. Ali also informed her that Kamande had problems with his eyesight but that he kept cows, sheep and goats on the land that she had obtained for him in Dagoretti, on the outskirts of Nairobi.

In her book *Notater om Karen Blixen,* Clara Selborn mentions a couple of 'strictly confidential' drawers in 'Ewald's room' at Rungstedlund, in which Karen Blixen kept important papers and letters. In these drawers were also the letters from Farah and the other staff members from the farm, along with a list of names of the people in Africa who were to inherit from her after her death.

Karen Blixen drew up a will in 1936, in which all her staff from the farm would inherit something after her death. At the same time, she mentioned 127 squatters, who were each to receive 50 shillings to buy themselves a sheep. Seven squatters who owned nothing were each noted to receive 100 shillings, and a big ngoma was to be held for all the heirs, for which was set aside £100. This will was altered after Farah's death, as Karen Blixen had counted on him to take care of the organization of this ngoma and to be able to trace all the recipients of her bequests.

Karen Blixen occasionally received news from travellers who had talked to her former farm workers. A Danish journalist and Karen Blixen's friend, Helge Christensen, carried news from Juma and Kamande when he met them during a visit to Kenya in 1950. He described this meeting in a small booklet called 'Juma and Kamande'.

The author John Buchholzer describes in his book *The Horn of Africa* a visit to northern Somalia. One day, he attempted to photograph people in a marketplace in Hargeisa. They became angry and threw stones at him, but the young Somali who accompanied him rescued him and brought him safely back to his hotel. The following day, he received an unknown visitor who had been told that Buchholzer was Danish.

'I have heard that you come from Denmark', said a Somali to me. 'Do you know Baroness Blixen? How is she? Is she still alive?'[32]

He introduced himself as Abdullahi

Ahmed, and told the following story about himself:

'Farah Aden, who was the Baroness's house-boy, was my cousin and I went to the farm when I was a lad. I helped Farah in the Baroness's house, and I was very happy. She was like a mother to me, and yes, she was a mother to us all. She made no difference between white and black, and she was loved by black and white people alike. She saw that I went to school in Mombasa. She paid for me to go there and I shall never forget her for that. It was sad for all of us when she left the farm. I came here to Somaliland and became a writer of complaints and applications. In those days there were few of us who could either read or write. There was a lot of work, with all the complaints and applications to the Administration to be written. Often I worked till far into the night, and I used to think, "If only I had a typewriter!" Then I wrote to the Baroness in Denmark and asked her if she could help me with one. And shortly afterwards she sent me one. Gradually I got better and better jobs in the Administration, and now I am a magistrate.

'I have the Baroness to thank for all this. You understand how grateful I am? And do you understand how glad I am to meet a fellow countryman of hers? Tell her, please, that there are many of us who still remember her. She would weep, if she saw what is happening in Kenya today. She was a lady and we looked up to her and we loved her. That is why we who know her think that all people from Denmark are good and that they are people who understand us.'[33]

John Buchholzer carried the letter on page 31 with him back to Denmark and sent it to Karen Blixen with the following note:

29.2.56

Dear Mrs. Karen Blixen,

During my travels through the Somali countries, where I especially studied folk-poetry, I met Abdullahi Ahmed, who was deeply moved to hear some news about you.

The boy, who you once helped to go to school in Mombasa and later, when he had become application-writer in Somalia, sent a typewriter, has now become a big man—judge—in Hargeisa. I enclose a letter from him.

With kind regards,

Yours John Buchholzer

When the young American photographer Peter Beard contacted Kamande and Abdullahi in 1962, at the request of Karen Blixen, he became a new link in the chain that connected Karen Blixen to her old friends in Africa. He had just visited Karen Blixen in Denmark and promised to get information for her about those who might still be alive, and to let her know how they were.

In October 1964, Karen Blixen's brother, Thomas Dinesen, came to Nairobi with his wife. It was the first time in forty years that he had set foot on African soil, since living on the farm in 1924. He had come on a special

Kamande, Peter Beard and Abdullahi Ahmed Weid, 1969.

When Peter Beard came to Kenya in 1962, he had recently visited Karen Blixen in her home in Rungstedlund, Denmark, and she sent through him her warmest greetings to her African friends. Peter Beard was able to trace Kamande and Ali bin Hassan. Later, he sent an airline ticket to Abdullahi, who lived in Somalia, asking him to come to Nairobi. Here they are photographed at Hog Ranch, Peter Beard's home, with the Ngong Hills in the background. Abdullahi is on the right.

errand on behalf of his sister. He invited Kamande Gatura, Ali Hassan, Ahmed Farah Aden (Sofe), and Mohamed bin Juma (Tumbo) to meet with him at the Norfolk Hotel, where he was staying. The reunion was marked by great happiness and teary smiles, and thankfulness that Karen Blixen had left 5,000 Danish kroner to five of her most cherished staff, or their children, in her will. Abdullahi, who was one of the heirs, was unable to attend as he lived in Hargeisa, Somalia.

Abdullahi came to Kenya in 1969, having received an invitation and an airline ticket from Peter Beard, who asked him to come to Nairobi for an interview about Karen Blixen. At that time, Abdullahi told one of the local papers, the *Sunday Nation,* how he left Hargeisa immediately only to find on his arrival in Kenya that Peter Beard had flown to the United States to be treated for hepatitis. During the five months he was away, Abdullahi waited patiently in Kenya, where he fortunately had family with whom he could stay. In addition to Kamande and Abdullahi, Peter Beard also traced Ali Hassan and Juma's son Tumbo. In 1975,

Letters 1931–1962

Peter Beard's book *Longing for Darkness* was published. In it, he renders Kamande's memoirs about life on Karen Blixen's farm. She never saw the book, as she died on 7 September 1962.

Karen Blixen kept most of her letters, among them the ones from her former staff and from her Nairobi solicitor, W.C. Hunter. He described in the letters he sent to her how he had executed her detailed instructions for the distribution of her money to the former staff from her farm, and they would send their thanks. I have copied some of these letters here, because they so clearly show how important it was for Karen Blixen to be able to continue to help her African friends.

Letter to Karen Blixen from Juma Bin Mohamed

2nd April 1935
Nairobi

Baroness Blixen
Rungstedlund
Rungsted
Kyst Denmark

May hon Baroness.

I have the hon to inform you that we have received your letter and Thanks to heard from you in about the healthy of our Mother and Mr. T. Dinesen and his family.

I further inform you that may son Tumbo always thinking you and with all your family and constantly asked me if I write to you <u>must</u> not forget the warm affection to you our old mother.

I therefore have went to miss Peacock and received my share without any Difficulty & I was pleasant through we all Pray to you always.

We thereby should be surprised if we always heard from by each Post.

In about Kenya we are little better for crops. This and we Expecting more rain with help of heavenly O. God: All may family Salaam to you and mother + Mr. T. Dinesen and they advise that write every week and must know how you getting on there as well Mother and T. Dinesen and your relative.

I should be very much delighted if I can have a watch and raincoat. Your child still in Mohamed school.

Excuse Madame.

I am your obedient servant.

Juma bin Mohamed,
P. O. Box 802
Nairobi.

Letter to Karen Blixen from W. C. Hunter

Muthaiga Country Club, Nairobi
Kenya Colony
P.O. Box 181
Jan. 13th. 1937

Dear Baroness von Blixen

Thank you for your letter of December 9th. which I only got about a week ago. Of course I will give out the money, as you ask. I cashed your cheque a few days ago and the money is already in the Club safe here. I have delayed writing you because I have been hoping to have seen Farah Aden before doing so: unfortunately he was away on safari but I understand he will be back in a few days. Though I do not know for how long. I have arranged that he gets a message to come and see me as soon as he comes back, when I will endeavour to arrange a day when he can bring all the boys mentioned in your letter of instructions. Please do not think it is any trouble. I will write again after I have seen Farah. As regard helping you with various small shauries you still have in Kenya I will gladly do this, but the trouble is that my wife & I hope to go on leave on March 12th. and we shall not be back until the middle of October. If I can be of any use despite that absence of 7 months, I will gladly do my best to help you. I will take down & send you any messages to you from your Boys. With kindest regards from my wife & myself. I am glad we may see you in Kenya again.

Yours very sincerely,
Wilfred C. Hunter

Letter to Karen Blixen from W.C. Hunter

Muthaiga Country Club
P.O. Box 181, Nairobi
Kenya Colony.
February 1st 1937.

Dear Baroness von Blixen,

With further reference to your letter of December 9th, I have at last managed to get hold of Farah Aden and to-day I have paid out on your behalf, the following:

Farah Aden. £5. He says 'Thank you very much and hopes you are well and he will see you again in Kenya.'

Juma Mohamed. £ 2. He thanks you very much and says his news is good.

Ali Hassan. £2. He thanks you very much and was evidently very pleased with your gift.

Kamante Gaturra. £2. He says' Thank you very much, his news is good, but two of his children have died.

Saufe Farah. £1.Says 'I thank you very much for all your kindness and says 'Salaam Sana'.

Tumbo Juma. £1. says 'Thank you very much and asked for news of you'.

Kamau. (Syce) £1. This I had to give to Farah who faithfully promised to give it to him as it is very difficult for him to get away.

Kinuthia £1. I have had to keep this in the hope of seeing him as he is in Kakamega, but Farah thinks he may be down before the end of February. I know you particularly wanted news of him.

Kinanjui Gun-bearer is dead.

I gave two shillings each to Ndwetti Goi Goi, Titi and Wamai who all wished me to thank you. Muthaiga could not come but Farah promised to see he got the money: he also promised to give 10/- which I gave him to the Syce to Poor-Box who could not come himself. Chota, the blind boy who worked in the garden will I hope come to see me when I will give him 10/-.

So I still have to pay Kanuthia £1. and Chotha 10/-: and I gave Farah the 10/- for the old blind Kikuyu woman who can not come herself. This means I have disbursed for you Shs 350/-. I have still to give out shs 3/- and then I shall have shs 15/- over: to whom shall I give this?

Yours sincerely,
W. C. Hunter.

P.S. Shall I return the Shs 15/- which will be over to you or would you like me to give it to someone else?

W.C.H.

Letter to Karen Blixen from Tumbo Mohamed

Bwana Dick
Ngong
8.6.38

To my
Dear Baronesse Von Blixen

Please I wish to Inform you that I am Very well then I have received your greeting from Ali & I Very Glad to hear if you are All right & I am now I am big man I can do any work but I still In school & I think I will be happy If you are coming to Kenya a visit year I should
YOU WILL SEE PICTURE IN THE ENVELOPE

[this is written at the bottom of the first page in the letter. The second page is missing, but the third page continues as follows:]

will help for your boy.

Give Bwana Thomas my Compliments & bwana Kidogo & Memsahib Mzee.

Good buy

I thanking you

All time God will save you in Europe.

Your Little boy
Tumbo Mohamed.

Letter to Karen Blixen from Farah Aden

c/o The Shariff Ishak
Community,
P.O. Box. No. 1483,
Nairobi,
10th, February, 1939,

Baroness Blixen,
Rungstedlund,
Rungsted Kyst,

Madame,

I am in receipt of, and thank you very much indeed for your very kind gifts.

I have received the 200/- personally myself and Saufe have also received his own 50/-, this was received through Mr. W.C. Hunter, who has paid all your old boys the bukshishi you sent for us all.

I am sorry to say that I have been very ill, I was in bed for over one month but I am much better now.

Undoubtedly, I will never forget your kindness because I always receive your help when I am in need.

I shall esteem it a very great favour if you will convey my very best salaams to your mother, Mr. Thomas, his Memsahib and the children.

I am glad to hear that you intend to come to Kenya, how very lucky I shall be?

I pray the Almighty God to be always with you and for your very long life and very high propserity [sic].

Salaams to you from Saufe and all my family.

Hoping to hear from you very soon.

Your most obedient,
Farah Aden.

Letter to Karen Blixen from Abdullahi

Hargeisa
25th. July 1955.

Baroness von Blixen
Denmark

Dear Madam,

In fact, it is very disappointing to say that I neither hear from you nor you hear from me for a considerable time.

I never had any information since the last 10 years ago whether you are still alive or not. It was a remarkable occasion to me when I hear from this gentleman, a journalist from Denmark, that he knows you very well and that you are still living. I felt then to hasten and write this letter to you in order to inform you about me and about Farah Aden's family. About me, I am living in Somaliland, working in the capital as Judge of the subordinate court. I have been holding this capacity since the 3 1/2 years ago. I am carrying my official duty successfully with dignity and popularity. I am to proceed on leave with effect from 1st. August 1955, that is after 6 days. I am going to visit Kenya in order to see Farah Aden's family again. I received a letter from Sofe Farah Aden in which he wrote me that they are still all quite well. The letter was dated 31st May 1955. In it he informed me that his maternal grandmother (Ibado Awil) died on 30th. May 1955 in Nairobi.

Sofe Farah Aden has married the daughter of Halima Wirreh and he is now living with his wife and father in law at Kitale. On my arrival to Kenya I shall write to you and hope will be able to give you more news God willing about Farah's family from there. Although you may already hear I married Fatuma Barud, widow of Farah Aden according to the Somali custom and that she got a son for me who is now about 10 years old.

In Somaliland, I got two sons and a daughter. Both my two sons are in secondary school in Somaliland. One in the 9th. standard and the other in 8th. standard. The daughter is 3 years old. I lost 4 boys and 4 daughters in Somaliland.

My dear madam how happy I was when I heard that you are still living. Honestly I cannot find words how to express our gratitude towards the help you rendered to me and my deceased's cousin's family. As we have nothing to recompense to you I pray to almighty God to recompense you for the same.

If you could write to me please address as follows:

Mr. Abdillahi Ahmed
c/o Sheikh Farah Dusleh
P.O. Box 113 Kitale
Kenya Colony.

Yours obediently
A. Ahmed.

Letter to Karen Blixen from Ali Hassan

Ali Hassan
c/o Ndiloi Farm
P.O. Subukia,
Nakuru, Kenya.
Tel. Subukia 5y3.

Dear madam,

I am very happy and glad too, to see your photo.
Really it made my heart to be very pleased that I have written to you and remember you.
I have been remembering you and I shall remember you in future until one dies.
It fills my heart with joy when I hear your name mention or when I mention your name.
When remembering how you were kind to me I shall not forget you.
Lastly I beg whether you will find me a Denmark Wrist Watch. I shall be very pleased if you will get me one.
GOD BLESS YOU AND GIVE YOU LONG LIFE

Yours faithfully
ALI HASSAN

[The photo Ali Hassan refers to was a picture of Karen Blixen he had seen in a magazine.]

Letter to Kamande from Karen Blixen

RUNGSTEDLUND
Rungsted Kyst *19 July, 1962.*

My good and faithful servant Kamande,

I was glad to get your letter with the two photos and to learn that you and your family are well. I was also glad to hear about you from Mr. Peter Beard, and I wish I had been with you to my old house, so that we could talk of old days.

I am sending you a small present of money to help you a little in the bad times.

I am still living in the old house where I was born. It is very lovely here, and I am well.

Mr. Thomas is well, and he asks me to send you his greetings. He has got four children and six grandchildren. He is living not far from me.

I pray to God that you may be well, and that your children and your whole family may be in good health and have good luck. I wish that I could see you again.
So goodbye, Kamande.

Baroness Blixen.

Five

Farah Aden

'Farah was a highly picturesque figure in my house as he stepped forth on its threshold.'[34]

When Karen Blixen first travelled to Africa in 1913, her mother and her sister Ellen accompanied her as far as Italy. From there, she travelled alone by ship to Kenya. Bror Blixen was already in Kenya and had promised to meet her in Mombasa, but as she went ashore in Aden, the last stop before reaching Mombasa, a Somali was waiting for her with a letter from Bror. The Somali introduced himself as Farah Aden, and in the letter, Bror told her that he was 'reliable and pleasant' and would help her on the last leg of her journey. Karen Blixen wrote to her mother from the boat that she now had an 'Indian servant':

'He was really pleasant, smiling and greeting me with his hand to his forehead, extremely respectably dressed, but he spoke English badly and also had such a terrible stammer that he seemed about to die every time he tried to speak.'[35]

During the following seventeen years, Farah gradually became Karen Blixen's intimate friend, so much so that when they parted on the quay in Mombasa for the last time in 1931, she felt as if her right hand was being amputated.

Karen Blixen soon realized that Farah was not an Indian but a Somali of the Habr Yunis tribe, a proud Mohammedan, and a man of many talents.

Farah Aden, in 1917.

When Karen Blixen lay in bed with a fever shortly after her arrival in Kenya, she wrote in a letter to her Aunt Bess: 'Fara is my great comfort and support, better than a white lady's maid and so thoughtful and sensible, and then the Somalis have a bearing like Spanish grandees.'[36]

In *Shadow on the Grass,* Karen Blixen described Farah's position in the house as follows:

'When Farah first took service in my house, or first took my house into possession — for from that day he spoke of "our house", "our horses", "our guests" — it was no common contract which was set up, but a covenant established between him and me *ad majorem domus gloriam*, to the even greater glory of the house. My wellbeing was not his concern, and was hardly of any real importance to him, but for my good name and prestige he did, I believe, hold himself responsible before God.'[37]

'In his relations to my native servants he was unwaveringly fair and impartial and he had a deeper knowledge of them and their course of thought than I could well account for, for I hardly ever saw him converse with them.'[38]

Karen Blixen on the farm with some of her staff members and their children, in 1930. From the left: Farah, his son, Sofe, Karen Blixen, Tumbo and Ali Hassan. In the background: Juma and Halima, Fathima's cousin.

Karen Blixen wrote about her staff before she left the farm in 1931: '. . . and then there are my black folk here. Until arrangements have been made for them.–as far as they can be made, and I don't know how good they will be,–I have neither the strength nor the time to manage to do anything for myself. You understand, they stay here the whole time and come running after me when I am walking or riding on the farm; they say: "Why do you want to go away? You mustn't go, what will become of us?'[39]

Farah Aden

During the 17 years Karen Blixen lived in Africa, she was a diligent letter writer, and in many of her letters she mentioned Farah's name in one connection or other. In her books *Out of Africa* and *Shadows on the Grass* Farah is mentioned often and always with respect and warmth. One could easily get the impression that Farah was always available when Karen Blixen needed him, as the following quotes would suggest:

'I had Farah with me as far as Marseilles, as I was rather ill when I left Mombasa, but sent him home from there.'[40]

'Farah came to meet me at Mombasa and it was really touching to see him again.'[41]

'Farah is standing here behind my chair engaging me in conversation whenever I put down my pen. When Bror is away we always have very pleasant evenings together; he tells me all news from Somali circles.'[42]

'I have Farah, who is truly an angel.'[43]

Perhaps Farah did not have much of a private life while living on the farm, but he was, in fact, often away either on private errands or with Bror Blixen on safari. Although Karen Blixen was very fond of him, he could at times really annoy her.

'Farah is *very* helpful, as you can imagine, and has put all his nonsense behind him and is a great comfort to me.'[44]

'. . . and when Farah has been in his sulky mood I have come to realise to what an extent I am reduced here, not merely as regards the normal congenial exchange of opinions but even the modest encouragement provided by what one calls "a kindly word"'.[45]

'At times Farah like most Somali annoyed me by having so little *Gemütlichkeit* in his mental make-up. I accounted for it by the tribe's abstinence from wine or spirits through a thousand years, and reflected that the sight of an old uncle dead drunk would have been a wholesome remedy against the desert dryness of the Somali mind.'[46]

'Farah can fall into the same type of fit and harp on his privileged misery as "only a coloured man", until I have to say "Stop that nonsense, now, Farah; you are much better off than I am".'[47]

Karen Blixen had many people employed in her house, and in time she got to know several of them intimately, but no one attained such a special place in her heart as Farah. She wrote to her brother, Thomas: 'Whatever comes to pass, please will you remember that Farah has been my best friend out here,—'.[48]

Most of Karen Blixen's English friends had, as she did, a personal Somali servant who was in charge of their housekeeping. On festive occasions, they would dress in the Somali national dress—a long white robe of silk or cotton, black waistcoat embroidered with gold, and a gaily coloured turban made up of a square shawl twisted around their heads in traditional fashion. Otherwise, they dressed in a long white robe with a simple waistcoat and turban, or European dress.

Karen Blixen spoke English with Farah but, as many of her staff members belonged to different Kenyan tribes who each spoke their own language, they communicated amongst themselves and with Farah in Kiswahili. Karen Blixen quickly learned this language with Farah's help, but it was he, as housekeeper, who took care of everything concerning the house and the staff, and it was he who made sure that the work was done. Farah was also responsible for Karen Blixen's stables, and he took care of all arrangements concerning her safaris. Travel companion, chauffeur, nurse and accountant were just a few of the titles he could, over time, add to his work description.

Every month, Karen Blixen gave Farah a fixed amount of money to finance the housekeeping, but he never produced any accounts to show how this money was spent, nor was he ever asked to produce any reconciliation. He carried all the keys to the house, and Karen Blixen trusted him blindly.

'I never doubted but that he did to the best of his ability spend my money in the interest of my house. Only there always remained to me a strong exciting element of suspense as to his views of the interests of the house.'[49]

'I have made a contract with Farah, for him to supply me with eggs, butter, meat, poultry and vegetables for £2.10 a week. I think he will make a profit out of it, but it will save me always having to get supplies, which is quite troublesome.'[50]

Hassan Ismail, who worked in the house under Farah, had a duka close to the farm, and it is likely that Farah shopped in Hassan's duka, as his own was very far from the farm. Farah, no doubt, had some extra income besides his wages from Karen Blixen during the years he worked on the farm, as almost all Somalis are clever businessmen. Karen Blixen wrote in 1926:

'Farah is going to take over Hassan's duca here at the end of the month, but will remain in my service. I am glad about it; it will mean that I can get all my stores and meat from him, and now his duca at Thika takes him away so much. Fat Abdullahi is to work in the shop for a year when he leaves school. Farah has bought himself a Chevrolet lorry and is very excited, as you can imagine . . .'[51]

One may well wonder how Farah combined his many chores in Karen Blixen's house with his own various businesses, as well as being away from the farm when he accompanied Bror Blixen on safari.

Farah and Karen Blixen had great conversations during the times she was alone on the farm, and even if she has said that the only thing they had in common was their age, they found many things to discuss. She wrote in *Shadows on the Grass*: 'In order to form and make up a Unity, in particular a creative Unity, the individual components must needs be of different nature, they should even be in a sense contrasts.'[52]

When Karen Blixen met Farah in Aden, in 1914, she felt sorry for him when she learned that he had been waiting for her arrival for a couple of weeks. She did not realize that he was born in Aden and had much family there. While he waited for the ship to arrive, he took the opportunity to marry his uncle's widow, Fatma Shire. It is custom in Somali circles that, after her husband's death, the widow marries a male member of the family, so that she and her children are supported and protected within the husband's family circle. Fatma already had a son by the name of Abdullahi, who was later brought to work on the farm by Farah. Nine months after her marriage to Farah, Fatma delivered a baby boy, and Farah asked for leave to go to Somalia.

'His restlessness has probably arisen because he has had a letter telling him that his wife in Somaliland has had a toto. We have long been looking forward to this event and counting on our fingers after my departure from Aden, as it was when he was there to meet me that he was married and the child was conceived, and now he is obliged to go out and earn some money for it.'[53]

Fatma Shire stayed in Somalia and, in 1918, Farah travelled to Mombasa to marry for the second time. He brought his new bride, Fatima, to Mbogani.

'Farah has gone to Mombasa to be married; he was in a rush to get it done before Ramadan, which is about to start with the new moon, and during which one must renounce all the joys of life, including doubtless those of love. I am having a house built for him, and my other Somalis are delighted at the prospect of having a young woman of their own race here.'[54]

Six weeks later, Karen Blixen wrote in a letter that she had Farah's and Hassan's wives for tea, and a couple of months later, in another letter written from Naivasha, she mentions that she left Farah in Nairobi so that he could celebrate his honeymoon with Fatima. Since then, Fatima seems to have disappeared mysteriously. Karen Blixen did not mention her again, and none of Farah's children had heard of her. They were of the opinion that Farah had married only twice.

Farah married for the third time in 1928, and Karen Blixen wrote about the new bride, Fathima Barud, in a letter home:

Pictured here are Fathima on the left with her first-born son, Sofe, her mother, Ibado Awil, in the middle and, according to Sofe, it is Halima on the right, who was later to become his mother-in-law (circa 1930).

When Farah married for the third time, in 1928, his new bride, Fathima Barud, arrived from Somalia accompanied by her mother, Ibado Awil, a younger sister and a cousin, Halima.

'Farah's wife has arrived and is very sweet; it is hard for the poor little thing in such utterly strange conditions, she cannot speak a word of Swahili, — Ali's young wife is giving her lessons in it,—and Farah I am sure is a terrible martinet.'[55]

'When Farah married, and brought his wife from Somaliland to the farm, with her came a lively and gentle little flight of dusky doves: her mother, her younger sister, and a young cousin who had been brought up with the family.'[56]

'The young cousin was married from the farm, in a pretty bungalow which was then empty, and which I lent to the Somalis for the occasion. The wedding was a splendid affair and lasted for seven days.'[57]

'Farah's son was born on the farm, Ahamed, whom they called Saufe, which means, I believe, a saw. In his heart there was none of the timidity of the Kikuyu children. When he was a tiny infant, swaddled like an acorn, with hardly any body to his dark round head, he sat up erect, and looked you straight in the face: it was like holding a small falcon on your hand, a lion-cub on the knee. He had inherited his mother's gaiety of heart, and, when he could run about, became a big joyful adventurer who held much influence in the young Native world of the farm.'[58]

Asha Farah Aden by 'Farah's Chest' at Rungstedlund, in 1993.

This picture of Farah's daughter Asha was taken during her visit to Rungstedlund. She is kneeling by the chest her father gave to Karen Blixen in Africa. Asha, who now lives in Canada, was in Copenhagen to visit her son at Rigshospitalet. She told me that he had been evacuated from Mogadishu, Somalia, to have a heart transplant in Denmark.

'Farah's wife was popular with the Kikuyu of the farm, and Kamante many times told me that she was very clever.'[59]

Apart from his son Ahmed, called Sofe (spelled by Karen Blixen as Saafe or Saufe),

Farah with four-year-old Sofe, and Abdi, born in 1932.

This picture was sent to Karen Blixen by Farah in a letter to her in 1933. He wrote once that he had bought a parrot as a present for her. 'When, he wrote, he had taught it a few more phrases and names of old mutual friends and acquaintances, if I was not coming back to Africa he would try to get it sent to Denmark. As in the end it proved to be impossible to realise this scheme, Farah gave the parrot to his mother-in-law, who all the time had much admired it, and sent me a few feathers plucked off it, to show me what colour it had been.'[60]

Farah had a daughter, Amina, born in 1930. Another son, Abdi, was born in 1932, the year after Karen Blixen left the farm. Ismail was born in 1937, then Ali, in 1939, Asha in 1940, and finally Khadija, in 1941.

Life on the farm was not always idyllic, as there were many quarrels amongst the staff.

'I always had Farah with me in my dealings with the Kikuyu, for while he showed but little sense where his own quarrels were concerned, and like all Somalis would lose his head altogether wherever his tribal feelings and feuds came in, about other people's differences he had wisdom and discretion.'[61]

'The Somali bring much trouble upon themselves by their terrible tribal quarrels. In this matter they feel and reason differently from other people. Farah belonged to the tribe of Habr Yunis, so that personally in a quarrel I sided with them. At one time there was a great real fight in the Somali town, between the two tribes of Dulba Hantis and Habr Chaolo, with rifle-shooting and fires, and ten or twelve people killed, until the Government interfered. Farah then had a young friend of his own tribe, by name of Sayid, who used to come out to see him at the farm, and who was a graceful boy, so that I was sorry when I was told by my houseboys that Sayid had gone round to visit a Habr Chaolo family in their house, when an angry member of the Dulba Hantis tribe had passed and fired two shots at haphazard through the wall of the house and broken Sayid's leg. I condoled with Farah on his friend's misfortune.—"What? Sayid?" Farah cried out with vehemence. "That was good enough for Sayid. Why must he go and drink tea in the house of a Habr Chaolo?"'[62]

In 1930, Karen Blixen wrote to her mother:

'We have had some entertainment lately from what Farah is convinced were three attempts to murder him. For a long time he has been at loggerheads with Hassan and his tribe and says that they have constantly threatened to kill him, and the other day when we were in Nairobi and Farah was waiting for me outside the Somali Hotel, one of them knocked him down with a stick and stabbed him in the back with a knife. The other night the dogs suddenly started to kick up a fearful din in the middle of the night, and when I went out to see what was the matter, I saw, —there was a faint moonlight, —two shadows running away from the neighbourhood of Farah's house. He said they had been shaking the door. This was repeated the following night, so I then gave Farah a gun and told him to fire off a shot if they came again. In the middle of the night the dogs started barking again, so I grabbed a pair of shoes to run out in, —bang went Farah's shot. Then there was a shout, but no one was lying on the battlefield when I went out, no blood was to be seen, but footprints of people in shoes all around Farah's house.'[63]

Kamande also remembers that Hassan's family came one night to Farah's house with knives and guns to kill him: 'Farah shot, and Juma came to his aid. Mrs. Karen then took Farah and Hassan to Nairobi to a Somali Judge, and later, she bought them each a duka.'[64]

Farah and Hassan both belonged to the Habr Yunis tribe and were originally very good friends, and when Hassan's first son, Mohamed, was born, he asked Farah to be the child's godfather. Some time later, however, they became such enemies that their differences could not be resolved, and they had to see a Somali judge.

Hassan Ismail's grandson, Abdi Mohamed Hassan, told me that after the case was tried the first time, Farah came out the winner and was awarded Hassan's duka. Hassan appealed the case and won the next round, and was given Farah's two properties in Eastleigh. Maybe Kamande was right when he said that it was Karen Blixen who finally cut the Gordian knot, by making sure that they both got a duka as, according to Abdi, Farah did not take over Hassan's duka near the farm.

When Karen Blixen first described Farah to her mother, she said that she hoped that Farah would not 'turn out to resemble Fara the Warrior'.[65]

Whether Farah was a 'warrior' can possibly be disputed, but he was a proud Somali, severe and unbending when he felt he was right, and he apparently often had one or two big cases in process. It was not only his own problems Farah had to deal with, but he also had to become involved when problems arose with his family in Somalia.

'Once the news came to Nairobi of how Farah's little brother, who was ten years old, in a place called Baramur, had taken up a stone and thrown it at a boy of a different tribe, knocking out two of his teeth. Over this matter representatives of the two tribes met at the farm to sit upon the floor in Farah's house and talk, night after night.

Old lean men came, who had been to Mekka and wore a green turban, arrogant young Somalis who, when they were not attending to really serious matters, were gunbearers to the great European travellers and hunters, and dark-eyed, round faced boys, who were shyly representing their family and who did not say a word, but were devoutly listening and learning. Farah told me that the matter was considered so grave because the boy's looks had been ruined, he might find it difficult, when his time came, to get married, and would have to come down in his pretensions as to birth or beauty in his bride. In the end the penance was fixed at fifty camels, which means half waregilt, full waregilt being one hundred camels. Fifty camels were then bought, far away in Somaliland, to be, ten years hence, laid on to the price of a Somali maiden, and to turn her eyes off the two missing teeth of her bridegroom; perhaps the foundation of a tragedy was laid. Farah himself considered that he had got off lightly.'[66]

To understand this way of meting out punishment, it is important to get an idea of how much a Somali loves his camels and his reluctance to part with even a single animal. Without camels, it is virtually impossible to survive the regular drought periods suffered in Somalia. The camel gives the Somali nomad everything he needs to survive the extreme and tough conditions of life in the desert, as it is able to endure very high temperatures and at the same time keep the balance of its body liquids constant. Milk production of the she-camel is unusual; she can produce twelve litres of milk a day and can be milked even eighteen months after giving birth. The milk is of such high quality that a human being can survive on it alone. Millions of Somalis owe their lives to their camels, as four litres a day is enough to keep an adult alive. The milk, which keeps fresh much longer than any other milk, is also rich in vitamin C. With all that in mind, it is not surprising that a man's wealth depends on the number of camels he owns.

When Karen Blixen left Kenya in 1931, Farah told her that he would settle in Somalia:

'Farah does not want to stay in Kenya but to go to Somaliland; but he has so many and varied interests here that must be wound up first. He has a big case on in Nairobi, which I have probably written to you about, but I think this is actually nearing a settlement now; but in connection with it my enemy Hempsted has contrived to have the permission for Farah to run his duca here withdrawn. I have been into Nairobi about that at least ten times. It is Hugh Martin who has the final say in this matter and it is never possible to get hold of him. In the end I ran him to earth at his house at eight o'clock in the morning, so that he couldn't escape, and I think it is in order now as far as the government permission is concerned, but now it remains to be seen what attitude the new owners will adopt towards it. It is unfortunate that when something collapses, like my ménage, it pulls so much down with it: Farah and Abdullahi have had a row, and Abdullahi has gone away without anyone knowing what has become of him, so I must set that to rights before I leave. In addition to all this we got involved in a cattle-robbing shaurie the other evening,—we caught some thieves as I was driving home after going to the farewell evening at the school,—which looks like taking up some time, and which

Juma, Farah and Tumbo on the boat at the time of Karen Blixen's departure, in 1931.

'Farah, by the time when I had to give up the farm and was leaving Africa, saw me off in Mombasa. And as I watched his dark immovable figure on the quay growing smaller and at last disappear, I felt it as if I was losing part of myself, as if I were having my right hand cut off.'[67]

Farah cannot get out of, although of course he is not suspected. Of them all it is Farah I am most deeply concerned about; he has been so extremely good in helping me with all kinds of shauries, but he has after all counted on his future being a part of mine, and I do want to help him and his family as much as I can.'[68]

Farah did not leave Kenya, and a few days before Karen Blixen left the farm, he moved his family and personal belongings to Eastleigh, a Nairobi suburb where many Somalis still prefer to live. He lived there for the rest of his life.

After Karen Blixen's departure, Farah was often away from Nairobi. This may be the reason why he and Fathima did not have any children from 1932 until Ismail was born in 1937. Farah often worked for Bror Blixen when he had clients on safari, and Sofe remembers that his father also worked as a driver for Major Thomas during the war, in the Northern Frontier District in Kenya, from 1940 to 1942. After that, he proceeded to Aden. When Farah had no other employment, he traded in cattle, sheep and goats.

Farah died suddenly in 1942 or 1943, from food poisoning, after dining in a restaurant with a friend. Karen Blixen did not learn of his death until the end of the war, and it upset her a great deal. He was buried at the Muslim Cemetery in Nairobi, but he had neither an impressive tombstone nor an epitaph, and the grave is today impos-

Farah's house in Eastleigh, to which he moved his family in 1931, when Karen Blixen left Kenya, still exists although it shows the ravages of time. Fathima Barud lived here until her death in 1972, and it has since then been occupied by Farah's son Ali. This photo was taken in 1995.

'My house-boys were still in the empty house, but they had, so to say, already moved their existence to other quarters, their families and their belongings had been sent off. Farah's women, and Saufe, had gone to the Somali village of Nairobi in a lorry the day before.'[69]

sible to find as it is unmarked. In *Shadows on the Grass*, Karen Blixen described how he helped her through the last difficult times on the farm and afforded him the most beautiful epitaph anyone could wish for:

'When during these months a visitor came to the farm, Farah stood forth, holding open the door to the empty rooms as if he had been doorkeeper to an Imperial palace. No friend, brother or lover, no Nabob suddenly presenting me with the amount of money needed to keep the farm, could have done for me what my servant Farah then did. Even if I had got nothing else for which to be grateful to him — but that I have got, and more than I can set down here — I should still for the sake of these months, now, thirty years after, and as long as I live, be in debt to him.'[70]

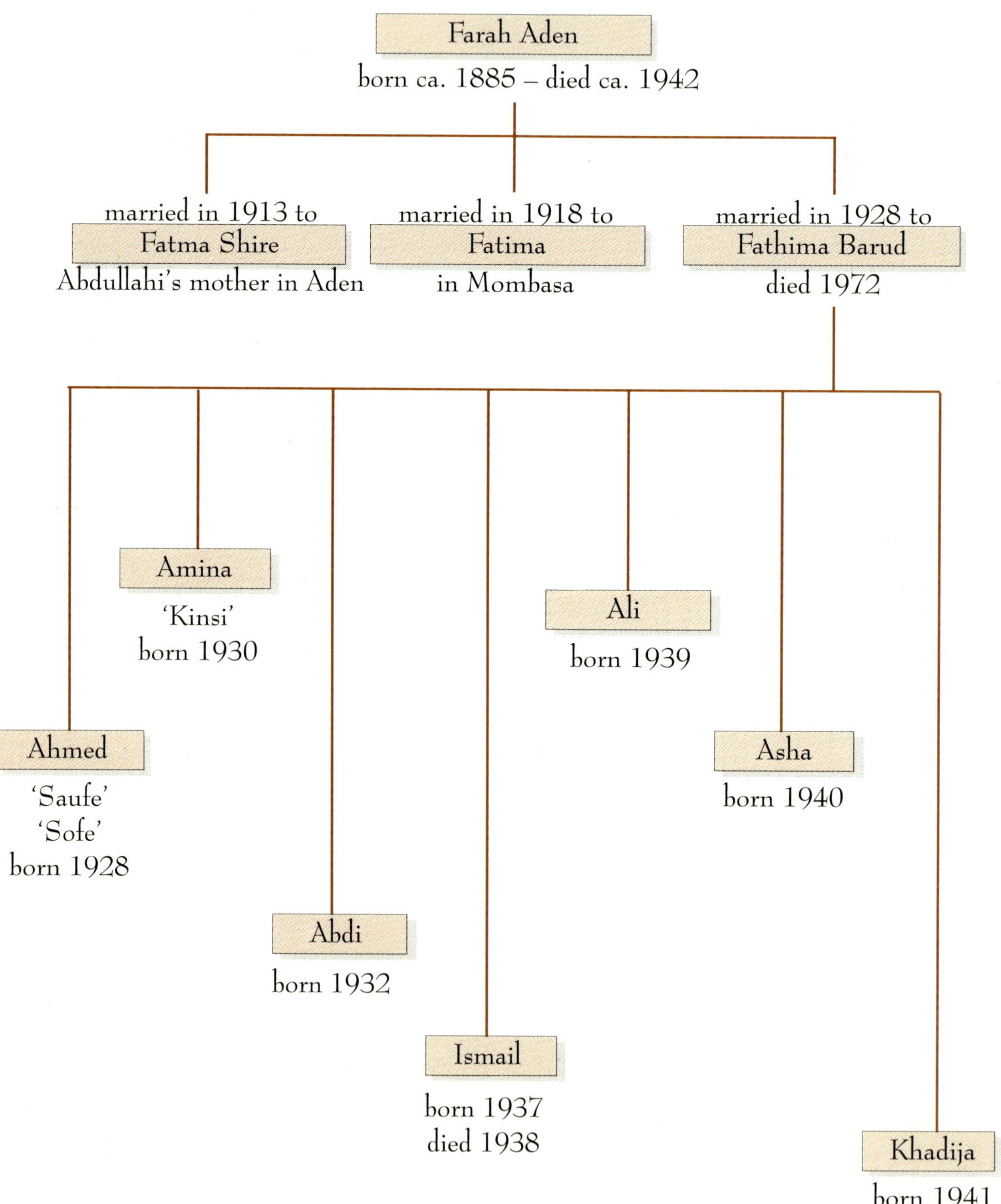
Farah Aden's Family
Farah Aden
born ca. 1885 – died ca. 1942
married in 1913 to
Fatma Shire
Abdullahi's mother in Aden
married in 1918 to
Fatima
in Mombasa
married in 1928 to
Fathima Barud
died 1972
Ahmed
'Saufe'
'Sofe'
born 1928
Amina
'Kinsi'
born 1930
Abdi
born 1932
Ismail
born 1937
died 1938
Ali
born 1939
Asha
born 1940
Khadija
born 1941

Six

Ahmed Farah Aden (Sofe – Saufe – Saafe)

'Saafe was so terribly sweet when I came home yesterday, deeply moved, he held my face in both his hands and would not let me go; they said he had been in utter despair when he came into the house and did not find me. This is a very happy love affair . . .'[71]

Farah's son Ahmed was born on the farm in 1928. Farah was of little or no use to Karen Blixen during the weeks leading up to the birth, spending most of his time in prayer and fasting. This was Fathima's first child and it was a very difficult birth. As the labour was drawn out and Fathima was suffering a great deal, Karen Blixen took Farah to Nairobi to fetch Dr. Sorabji, who was not in when they arrived at the clinic. As Karen Blixen had other errands to attend to, she left Farah to wait for the doctor's return. When they all returned to the farm about the same time, the child had just been born. They named him Ahmed, but as a baby he was nicknamed 'Shimbir', which means 'little bird'. Later he became known as 'Sofe', which means sharp (as the edge of a knife). He thinks he got this name because of the pain he caused during the difficult birth.

Sofe was the child which Karen Blixen found the most irresistible, and he was, as she herself expressed it, 'the apple of my eye'. Farah and Fathima had a daughter two years later, whom they named Amina, but she died as an infant. Karen Blixen thought that newly born Somali children were like small dolls, not 'unfinished' like European children, and she was convinced that Sofe had reached the height of his delightfulness when he was two years old.

Sofe claims to be the first black child in Kenya to be carried on the arm of a white woman, and Karen Blixen wrote this about him:

'Saafe is a great joy; I cannot describe how sweet he is. I have been suffering from such terrible nightmares that I have been quite terrified and have had him to sleep in my bed; it is so big that he quite disappears into it. I could not have the dogs, they make such a noise . . .' [72]

Sofe was too young to remember anything about his early years on the farm; neither does he remember the move to the new house in Eastleigh. But he does remember that his father was often away from Nairobi after they moved to Eastleigh, either on safari with white hunters, or trading between Kenya and Somalia. He also remembers visiting his father when he worked in the

Sofe is playing soldier with a friend on the farm, circa 1930.

'I am sending you a picture of Saafe to make up for the shortness of this letter. - You may think you have had enough of him by now, and perhaps the pictures do not show how really enchanting he is; but he plays a big part in my life and is a great joy. He hasn't really got such a stomach as he appears to have in the photograph, but he is an Askari and has adopted a military stance; he is an incredibly funny mimic; now that he has had his head shaved he is Denys and comes in saying: "Good-morning, good-morning", and is ready to die laughing over his roles.'[73]

Northern Frontier District, Kenya, during the first two years of the war, and that from there Farah continued to Somalia, before returning to Kenya. Farah was a strict father to his children and punished them with a beating if they were disobedient. 'He smacked his own small son Saufe because he repeated some words of abuse about the Virgin which naughty Kikuyu Totos from the Scottish Mission had taught him.'[74] Sofe clearly remembers a thrashing he had from his father once; he had played with a boy from another tribe in spite of his father's strictest prohibition.

Sofe was about 14 years old when Farah died. It was a hard blow for the family,

Ahmed Farah Aden, 'Sofe', in February 1994.

'The Somali are very handsome people, slim and erect as all East African tribes, with somber, haughty eyes, straight legs and teeth like wolves. They are vain and have knowledge of fine clothes. When not dressed as Europeans—for many of them would wear discarded suits of their masters from the best London tailors and would look very well in them—they had on long robes of raw silk, with sleeveless black waistcoats elaborately embroidered in gold. They always wore turbans of the orthodox Mohammedans in exquisite many-coloured cashmeres, those who had made the pilgrimage to Mecca might wear a green turban."[75]

especially Fathima, who found herself left with six small children, four of whom were below the age of six. Sofe was sent to Karamoja, in Uganda, to stay for a while with Sheikh Farah Duale and work in his shop. Upon Farah's death, Abdullahi assumed the role of head of the family and, according to Somali custom, came to Kenya to marry the widow, Fathima. He, however, returned to live in Hargeisa, northern Somalia, where he already had a wife and two children. Fathima stayed in Eastleigh for the rest of her life.

After Sofe had been in Uganda for about nine months, Fathima sent for him to return and find employment in Kenya where the war was still going on. One of Sofe's friends worked in a British Army workshop, and he arranged for Sofe to try for an apprenticeship there. First, he had to pass a test in which he was shown a screwdriver, and asked to tell about it. Sofe, who had been thoroughly prepared by his friend, answered correctly and was also able to identify the next tool he was shown; he passed the test and was granted the apprenticeship. He also learned to drive a car during the time he worked for the British Army.

There were several Italian prisoners of war at the workshop and, as they were not allowed outside the military compound, they used Sofe to run their errands in town. He sold various goods in the market that were produced by the Italians in the camp, such as drinking glasses, metal trunks and lighters. Sofe received a percentage of his sales, and the drinking glasses sold especially well, as there was a shortage of these during the war. The glasses were made by filling empty beer bottles halfway with oil, which was then heated by inserting a white-hot metal rod in the bottle. When the oil became hot, the bottle broke at the level of the liquid, splitting the bottle into two parts. The bottom part was used as an ordinary drinking glass, while the top part, with its bottleneck sealed and a metal plate attached, made a useful wine glass.

Most of Sofe's earnings went to his mother, and the family invested money in cattle. In this connection, Farah's acquaintance with Karen Blixen came in handy, when the authorities suddenly decided that cows were no longer permitted to live in Eastleigh. As the cattle owners were not given enough notice to sell their cattle, it was decided that Sofe and Fathima should personally deliver a letter to Karen Blixen's old friend, Sir Philip Mitchell, requesting an extension of the time limit. When Fathima explained who she was, Sir Philip not only extended the time limit but also made sure that they were guaranteed a fair price at the abattoir. Sofe's brother Ali told me that they had 150 head of cattle at one time, and that the milk from these was poured into glass bottles, which were then delivered to the Indian *dukas*. Ali also remembered Karen Blixen's letters, which always contained money. She once sent money that was to be used to buy clothes for Sofe.

Ahmed Farah Aden together with his wife, Safiya, and mother-in-law, Halima, in 1995.

Halima, who came to the farm with Fathima's wedding procession in 1928, is today living with her daughter and son-in-law in Kitale, western Kenya.

'The cousin was a pensive girl with red-brown eyes, she could read Arabic and knew passages of the Koran by heart. She was of a theological turn of mind, and we had many religious discussions and talks about the wonders of the world.'[76]

Ahmed Farah Aden

Halima, who came to Kenya in 1928 with Fathima, was married on the farm, where her eldest daughter, Safiya, was born. She was nearly the same age as Sofe, and when the war ended, they were married in Kitale, where they still live, together with Safiya's mother. Sofe, who first traded in horses and cattle there, eventually started a small hotel and butchery together with his father-in-law.

There is no doubt that it was Sofe's natural charm, energy and business acumen that brought him success in life, but it was the Italian prisoners of war who boosted his career as a businessman when he discovered how fond they were of bananas. Sofe would buy ten bananas at the market for one rupee and then sell them to the Italians for one rupee apiece; this exchange was to everyone's great satisfaction.

Sofe married only once, and his eleven children have done well. The youngest is still in school and lives at home, but the others are scattered over a great part of the world. His oldest daughter works in Washington, DC; others live in Toronto, Canada, and a son has settled in the United Arab Emirates. The others still reside in Kenya. Sofe's ambition has always been to educate all his children well.

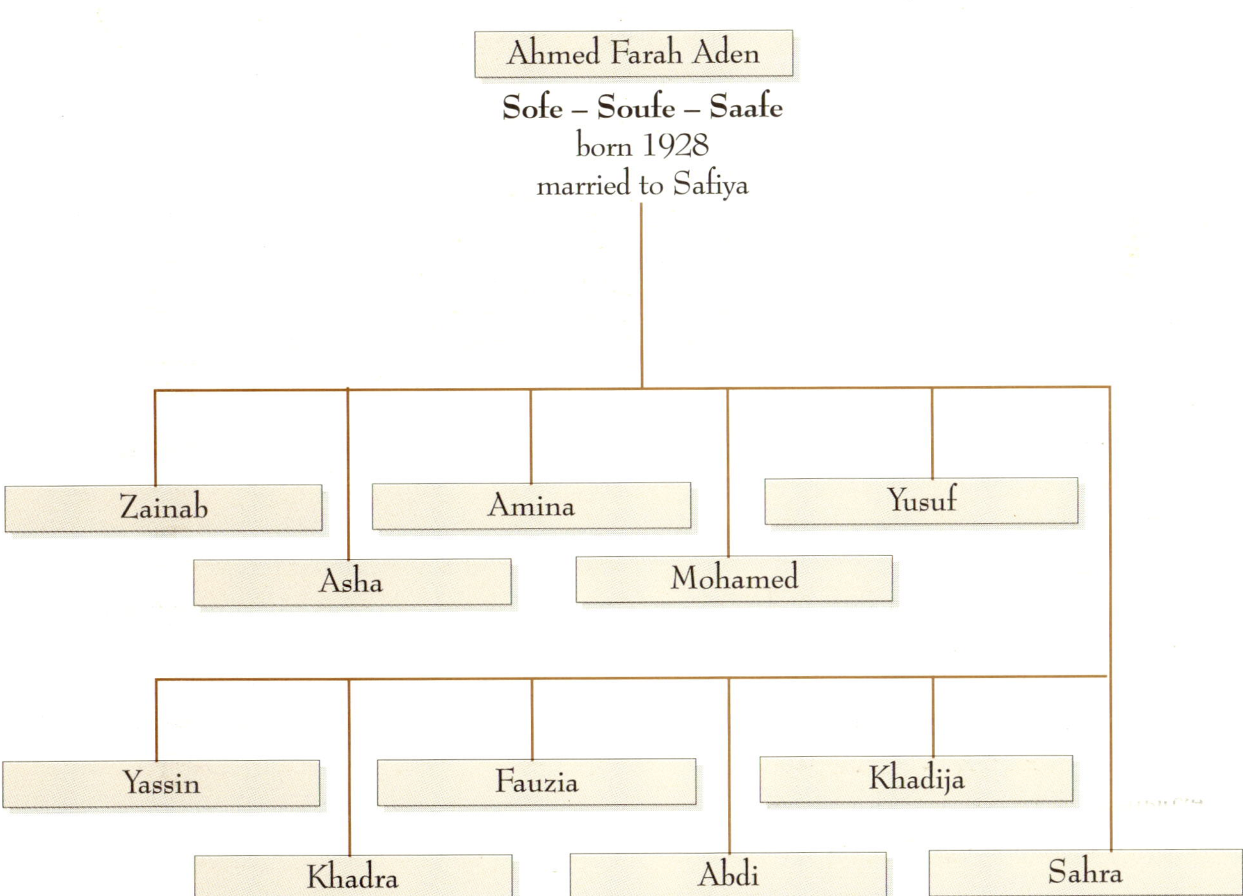

Seven

Abdullahi Ahmed Weid

Abdullahi Ahmed Weid, Farah's cousin, in 1917.

When Farah travelled to Aden in December 1912 to meet the ship carrying the young Karen Dinesen to Africa, he took the opportunity to marry his uncle's widow, Abdullahi's mother. He later brought her son to the farm, and Abdullahi has described his first meeting with Karen Blixen in a manuscript which he, unfortunately, did not get published before he died. The following is an extract from this manuscript:

'I Meet Baroness Blixen and Join Her Household.

'In the very evening of the day we arrived at Mombasa we took a train for Nairobi, arriving early the following day. Two days later Farah, who was employed as a domestic by Baroness Karen Blixen, went to see her at Ngong Road.

'Farah had overstayed his leave. However, since he had joined the Somali Levy and British forces which had launched an offensive against the dervishes, the Baroness overlooked his late return. He had worked for the Baroness' husband prior to their marriage. The couple had separated during Farah's absence.

'Farah took me to the Baroness' farm which was called Karen Coffee Company. She was the principal shareholder. She was pleased to see me since I was a relative of one of her helpers. She took me on as a chokra, a sort of personal boy, to work under Ali Hassan who was her personal boy. I can still remember the household: Hassan Ismail, the cook; Ali Hassan, Juma Mohamed, the table boy, and Kamande, the kitchen boy, who later replaced Hassan Ismail. Farah was the steward in charge of the domestic affairs of the household.'[77]

Abdullahi Ahmed Weid

Karen Blixen describes Abdullahi in *Shadows on the Grass*:

'Abdullahi had a round chubby face, an unusual thing in a Somali, and self-effacing manner, behind which one guessed weightily latent reserves. He was a loyal servant to the house, particularly pleasant to me because he was personally so clean and neat, and because I found in him a rare talent for gratitude. His individuality first manifested itself in an unexpected skill as a chess-player. He stood by, quiet as a mouse, while Denys and Berkeley, who both considered themselves superior players, sat by the board. When questioned he told them that he knew the game of chess, and when, experimentally, they took him on as an opponent, he played in unbroken silence and almost invariably won his game. Later I found him to be a talented arithmetician as well. Denys had left an *Oxford Book of Arithmetics* in the house. If I read out to Abdullahi one of its problems: 'Divide up a number in four parts, so that the one part plus 4, the second part minus 4, the third part multiplied by 4, and the fourth part divided by 4, will produce the same result,' he sank into a kind of dumb ecstasy, and the next day would bring me the solution without being able to explain how he had arrived at it.'[78]

Abdullahi's greatest wish was to go to school, and Karen Blixen wanted to help him achieve this. However, the nearest Muslim school was in Mombasa and it would be a costly affair. She could not spare the money at the time, so she had to tell Abdullahi that she could not afford it. He accepted this, but in spite of her explanation, he would still ask regularly if she had enough money yet. In 1923, she managed to raise the money for his school fees, and sent him off to Mombasa.

'Now Farah and I have sent little Abdullahi, Farah's brother, to school in Mombasa, —I am contributing a certain sum monthly to keep him there. He is a joy to us; his teachers praise him and say that he is industrious and eager to learn.'[79]

Abdullahi describes in his manuscript the circumstances concerning his schooling:

'After I had been at the farm about two years the Baroness raised the question of my education with Farah. They both agreed that I should be sent to school. The Baroness promised to pay half of my school fees. In 1923, Farah placed me in Buxton High school in Mombasa under the care of Khamiki, a Swahili friend. True to her promise, she paid half the cost. On some occasion when Farah could not pay his half, she paid more. In 1924 the Baroness suggested that Farah place me in the Church Missionary Society school in Nairobi, which was nearer home. She brought me a bicycle, so that I would be able to live at the farm. The next year she decided to visit her father in Denmark. Her brother, Mr. Thomas Dinesen, asked Farah to join him in a tour of Somaliland. Farah agreed and planned that, on the termination of the tour, he would stay in Somaliland and marry.

'The Baroness did not forget my education and undertook to pay fees of 120 shillings a month. I was to continue in the school at Nairobi, returning home daily to keep an eye on her house.

'She returned to Kenya after three months and soon afterwards Farah followed with his new wife.'[80]

As Karen Blixen's father had died when she was 10 years old, one has to assume that Abdullahi may have forgotten or been ignorant of this when he wrote that Karen Blixen was visiting her father. It was, of course, her mother she was visiting. Farah and Thomas Dinesen's safari in Somalia took place in 1923, but the wife Abdullahi mentioned must be Fathima, who arrived at the farm in 1928.

Abdullahi spent all his holidays on the farm, where he helped Karen Blixen in many different ways. She wrote to her brother that she planned to send Abdullahi to meet him and Ingeborg Dinesen on their arrival in Mombasa.

'The other Abdullahi, Farah's brother, is taking his final examination next month; it is high time for me, as in the course of time I have paid more than 1200 shillings on his

Karen Blixen's oil painting of Abdullahi, painted in 1923.

'Through these years I also kept up a correspondence with Abdullahi, my Somali servant, who by now was back in his own country. I have only mentioned Abdullahi very briefly before. Still he had for some years been a picturesque figure on the farm, with his own colours to him. I feel that he ought by now to be brought into the picture.'[81]

education—I hope it will be of use to him. He is indescribably big and fat, but his face is exactly as it was when he was six years old; he is a remarkable young fellow with his passion for learning, particularly for anything to do with mathematics; he is highly esteemed among the Somalis, especially because he is never kali, and Farah says that even old Somalis ask his advice in their disagreements. Perhaps he is going to turn into a kind of Solomon.'[82]

When Abdullahi finished school, he worked in Farah's duka near the farm. In between, he also functioned as mediator and adviser for the Somalis in Nairobi.

While Abdullahi lived on the farm, he once nearly killed Karen Blixen accidentally. She was prescribed three drops of arsenic for her illness, which she would mix in a glass of water before each meal, and one day she asked Abdullahi to fetch it for her. Without looking at it, she drank the whole content of the glass, instantly realizing that it was undiluted arsenic, a fact that Abdullahi did not deny when questioned. Karen Blixen asked him to summon Farah, as she knew that this dose might be fatal. When the seriousness of the matter dawned upon Abdullahi, he ran to Farah and told him that

Abdirrahman and Said Ahmed, in 1996.

Two of Abdullahi's youngest sons. Abdirrahman, on the left, closely resembles his father.

he had killed Memsahib, and then disappeared from the farm. Fortunately, his prophecy turned out to be wrong, as Karen Blixen recalled reading once about a cure against arsenic poisoning, consisting of egg white and milk. Farah brought this concoction to her. She managed to swallow it and was convinced that it saved her life. It took three days for a Maasai moran, sent by Karen Blixen, to find Abdullahi and bring him back to the farm.

Before Karen Blixen returned to Denmark in 1931, she wrote to her mother that Abdullahi had left the farm without saying where he was going, because he and Farah had argued. She wrote in *Shadows on the Grass*:

'When I left the country, Abdullahi did not care to stay there any longer either, but went back to Somaliland. From there he wrote to me, and I wrote back. He had not got Kamante's gift of letter-writing, his epistles to Denmark, beyond the fact that he was alive, gave little but a firm determination to hold on to me.'[83]

Abdullahi settled in Hargeisa, in northern Somalia, where it was easy for him to find employment as he was one of the few educated Somalis at that time. He started work as a petition-writer, and through diligence and competence he gradually worked his way up the hierarchy within the administration.

Abdullahi's first wife, Baada, bore him a son in 1937, by the name of Hassan. They had a total of four children. After Farah's death, Abdullahi married Farah's widow, Fathima, with whom he had another son, Mohamud, in 1944. Abdullahi informed Karen Blixen of this marriage and about their son. He also wrote and told her about the death of Farah's mother. Karen Blixen wrote about Abdullahi and Fathima in *Shadows on the Grass*:

'These holiday visits after a year were rendered difficult by the fact that Farah married, so that it had become illegal for Abdullahi to stay beneath his roof. In Somaliland, as in jewry, when a man dies his younger brother marries his widow in order to raise up his seed, and I gathered that the close connection between a youthful brother and sister-in-law is considered dangerous as a possible incentive to fratricide. In a nation of such strict loyalty in family affairs the rule betrays a strange faith in the fatality of passion. I was sorry about the taboo, for I felt that Abdullahi and Fathima, of the same age and both cleareyed and easy-going, would have got on very well together *en tout bien honneur*.'[84]

Abdullahi's third marriage was to another widow, after a younger brother's death. With her he had a daughter, Amina, in 1955. His fourth wife, Asha, gave him five children.

Said, the second youngest of Abdullahi's many children, told me that his father eventually gained extensive knowledge about the law by corresponding with an Indian lawyer. In the end, his hard work and strenuous studies led to a position as judge, which he held until he started his own law firm. He retired in 1974, to write a book about the history, politics and culture of Somalia during the hundred years between 1870 and 1970, entitled 'Out of Somalia'. During the civil war, his political involvement landed him in prison, where he eventually died in 1984, without seeing his book published. The only remaining copy of the manuscript was then with a New York publisher, but it has been retrieved by his son Said.

Abdullahi's children have managed well for themselves. They are well educated, and several of them now live abroad. Hassan is a lawyer in Somalia. Ahmed has a degree in meteorology and works in Saudi Arabia, where he lives with his mother. Mohamud was trained in Russia and Cuba in agro-chemistry, specializing in sugar. Ismail is a civil engineer and lives in India, Farrah is an accountant in Canada, and Said, who is a Kenyan citizen, works for a humanitarian organization in Nairobi. He is very keen on researching the interesting background of his family.

The Baroness felt that all were equal and that justice and fairness was everyone's right. In those days, racial discrimination in that multiracial county was similar to a war in which there was no actual field combat. Baroness always pretended that racial discrimination was non-existent. She knew it existed but at the same time she knew she could do nothing to remedy the situation. She purposely avoided discussing it with anyone. Unlike the Europeans, the Baroness had many connections with the Somalis. She had a number of Somali domestic servants whom she treated more as friends than as servants. She also liked the Somali women very much. She attended almost every Somali wedding. The women called her Utiyah which means "of gentle outlook and soft feature." She very often wore the dress of Somali women.

~~There were~~ some Somalis ~~who~~ were not friendly with the Somali servants of the Baroness. ~~However,~~ although honestly speaking, ~~there was~~ no one from the Somali community as a whole, ~~who~~ was displeased with ~~Baroness~~ the lady herself.

I regard the Baroness as "my mother by adoption," and can never forget her kindnesses to me. When I first arrived in Kenya at the age of 10, she employed me as a chokra or a sort of personal boy. Two years later she took the initiative in sending me to school in Mombasa. Later, for my personal convenience,

Page 15 of Abdullahi's manuscript.

~~she entered me in school in Nairobi.~~ When she left for Europe in 1931, she left me a farewell gift of 200 shillings. In 1934 when I had established a petition-writing business in Burau in the former Somali Protectorate, she sent me a typewriter which was a great help to me in my business. After the success of her book, Out of Africa, in 1938, she sent me a ~~one~~ thousand shillings thus allowing me to share in her success. She remembered me in her will in 1963, by leaving me the sum of five thousand Danish francs. This was equivalent to 4000 shs. after ~~the government~~ tax deductions.

It is for these many acts of kindness that I consider her my mother by adoption.

Page 16 of Abdullahi's manuscript.

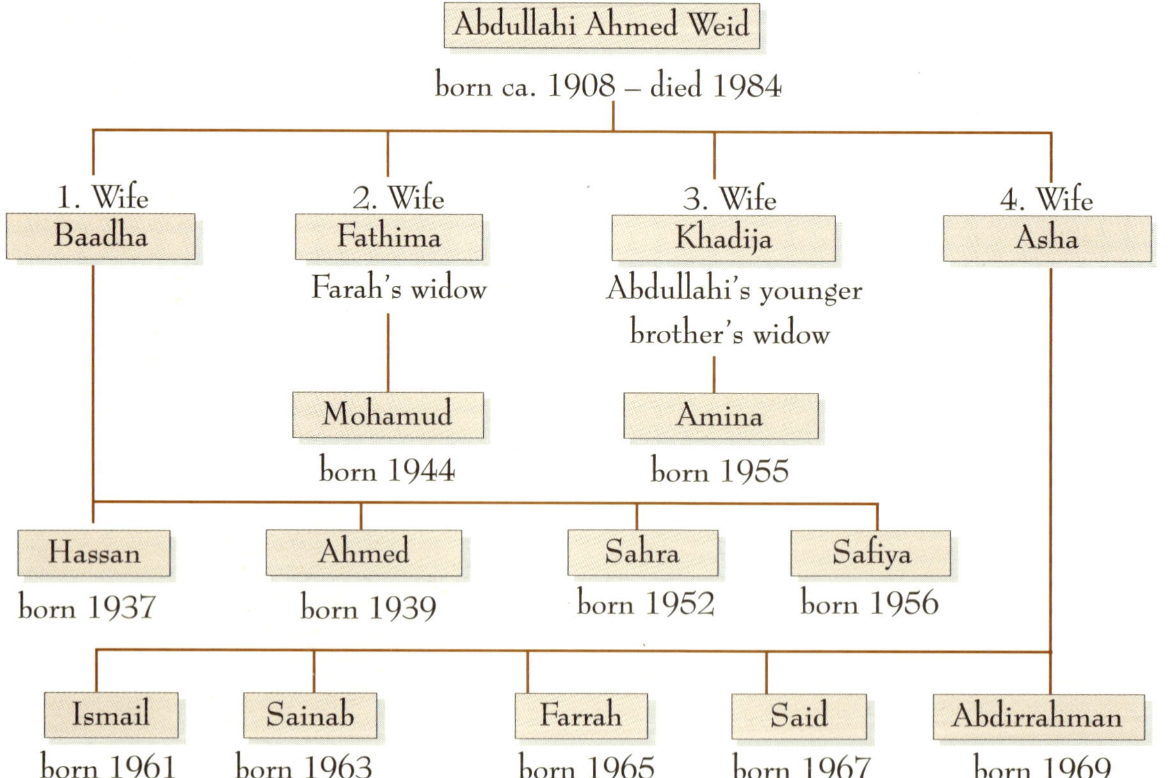

Eight

Hassan Ismail

Hassan Ismail was employed as a cook on Karen Blixen's farm in 1922, when the old cook, Esa, died. At an advanced age, Esa had married a much younger wife, whom he had difficulty keeping at home. Each time he fetched her back to the farm, she escaped again, and Karen Blixen was convinced that it was she who poisoned Esa in the end to get rid of him.

Hassan was newly married when he started to work at the farm, and he was already well established in business as a dukawallah in the area. He had one duka near the farm and two others in Dagoretti and Ngong towns.

In December 1922, Hassan's wife, Addo, gave birth to a son, whom they named Mohamed, and Farah became his godfather. Later, when Hassan and Farah became deadly enemies and it went so far that Farah feared for his life, Karen Blixen tried to mediate. When she did not succeed, she took the two adversaries to a Somali judge in Nairobi. The problem was still not resolved by the time she sold the farm, and in the meantime Hassan had moved to Ngong township with his family; his duka there exists to this day. He later moved to Juja, near Thika, where he set up another duka, which was subsequently combined with a small hotel and a butchery, a typical enterprise in the Somali business world at that time.

Hassan Ismail.

Hassan Ismail, circa 1922.

Hassan worked as a cook for Karen Blixen for four years. It was Hassan who, according to Kamande, slaughtered the cows and the game shot by Karen Blixen. He was the farm's official butcher, which was practical as Muslims will eat only meat that has been slaughtered according to Muslim custom. This picture was taken shortly after Hassan left Mbogani. The button in his waistcoat was a present from his former employer, Karen Blixen.

Hassan Ismail died in 1938 and left behind three sons and two daughters. The eldest son, Mohamed Hassan, was now forced to assume his father's role as head of the family at the tender age of sixteen.

Hassan's business in Juja was situated along the busy main road from Nairobi to Thika, opposite a farm belonging to a Swede, Ake Bursell. He was once Karen Blixen's manager but now had success as a farmer in his own right. When Mohamed Hassan's lease expired and he was asked to move, Ake Bursell gave him a piece of land on his farm across the road. A grateful Mohamed Hassan moved his whole business; it was an easy task as the buildings were mostly of wood and corrugated iron sheets, but solid enough to remain there until today.

The young Mohamed Hassan was forced to leave Alliance High School, where he had

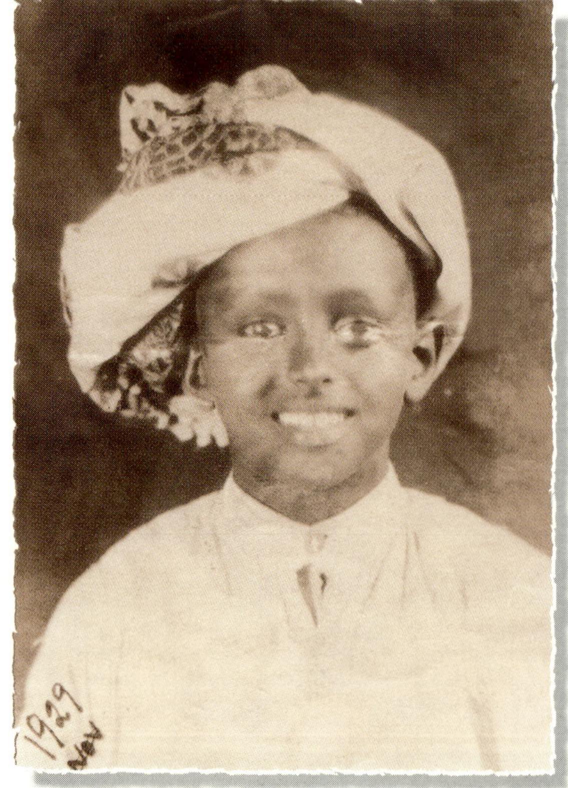

Mohamed Hassan, in 1929.

Addo and Hassan Ismail's oldest son, Mohamed, who is seven years old in this photograph. There is no doubt that he has inherited his mother's good looks. Karen Blixen, who loved children, found him irresistible.

Mohamed Hassan, circa 1938.

Mohamed Hassan was not only a beautiful child but also very intelligent. He became the first Muslim pupil to be admitted to the Alliance High School, Nairobi. Established in 1926, it was the first school in Kenya to give African students a chance of an education higher than that offered by missionaries. Many of Mohamed's schoolmates went on to become the future leaders of Kenya.

been a student, when his father died. He later became involved in politics and in 1944 was co-founder of the political party Kenya African Study Union, which was renamed the following year as Kenya African Union (KAU). Mohamed Hassan supported the Kenyan freedom fighters against colonial rule, for which he was briefly imprisoned in the fifties, accused of having supplied the freedom fighters with food and other supplies. His business was at the same time confiscated, but it was returned to him later. Today it is rented out.

Mohamed Hassan's eldest son, Abdi, was born on Ake Bursell's farm and was greatly indulged by his grandmother, Addo, whom he loved dearly and visited regularly until her death.

I met Abdi Mohamed in 1993, and he invited me to visit Addo in her house in the densely populated Eastleigh suburb. I had previously asked Abdi if he knew of anything Addo might still remember from the years she lived on the farm. On the way to her house, he told me that his grandmother had spoken often of Karen Blixen, but since she was now 95 years old, she was no longer as mobile and healthy as she had been a few years earlier. Karen Blixen wrote about Addo Hassan in a letter:

'I had Hassan's and Farah's wives here to tea yesterday. It is remarkable that although the Somalis are so completely civilized their

Abdi Mohamed Hassan, in 1993.

women are not so at all, —they are oriental, straight out of "A Thousand and One Nights". They are very beautifully dressed in silks and embroideries but creep about soundlessly like cats on their little bare feet, and they have such big flaming black eyes and white teeth; there is something of the big cat, lioness or leopard about them. I showed them all around the house, all my clothes (!), china, glass, etc., they were intensely interested and so tremendously lively, like children. Hassan's wife is a real beauty . . .'[85]

Many Somalis living in Kenya are in the transportation business, and big lorries with trailers dominate the streets in Eastleigh, as they are parked everywhere. Addo's house lay in an area known as Mlango Mkubwa (meaning 'the big door'), so named after a very rich man once built himself a large house there. I had to drive very carefully, avoiding some of the larger potholes in the tarmac on the very busy streets, where competition with other road users for the remaining tarmac was serious and intense. There were goats everywhere, browsing on the piles of garbage that lined the streets. Everything was drab and dusty, and the dull surroundings were intensified by the fact that nothing green broke the grey monotony. The

Addo Hassan, in 1993.

Hassan Ismail's wife, Addo, came to the farm together with her husband in 1922. She was then 24 years old, and expecting her first child.

In this photograph, she is 95—and still shows signs of her former beauty. She lived a long and active life, apart from the last few years when she rarely left her house in Eastleigh.

two-story building in which Addo lived looked like an oasis in the desert, and I was offered the luxury of a parking space under the only tree for miles. The front door was shining with fresh blue paint, and a narrow staircase led to the apartment on the first floor.

Abdi fetched his grandmother while I waited in the sitting room. She had been taking a nap after lunch and was accompanied into the room supported by Abdi's arm. I had been told that she once spoke English, but she had long since forgotten most of it, so we conversed in Kiswahili. I asked her during our conversation if she remembered Karen Blixen, and she answered:

'Now I am just an old woman and I have forgotten everything, but I remember that Memsaab Blixen was a nice lady of royal blood. She often came to visit the Somali women who lived on the farm and asked us many things. She invited us to her house for tea, and was very fond of children. She liked my first-born son, Mohamed, who was born on the farm in December 1922. Memsaab always carried him on her arm, whenever she met him.'[86]

While we were drinking tea, she told me about her children and her health and suddenly asked me if I was Bwana Thomas's daughter. 'He was such a nice man, and he

Museum director Marianne Wirenfeldt Asmussen, Asha Farah Aden and Fatuma Mohamed Hassan, in Copenhagen, in 1993.

I met Fatuma and Farah's daughter Asha at the home of Marianne Wirenfeldt Asmussen, the director of the Karen Blixen Museum in Denmark. When next I spoke with Fatuma, it was to bring her the sad news that her grandmother Addo had died.

promised me a present, when he left the farm.'[87]

I told her that Karen Blixen had described her in a letter as a real beauty when she was young. She laughed heartily and said that now she was only very old and no longer beautiful. As I photographed her, she smiled, and I could discern the previous beauty which her granddaughter, seated across from her, had inherited.

When tea was over, it was time for the next of the five daily Muslim prayers, and Addo was very tired.

'Remember me to everyone of Memsaab and Bwana Thomas's families and give them my fondest regards,' were Addo's final words to me when we bade farewell. She died in May 1995.

On the way back from Eastleigh, Abdi asked me where I had lived in Denmark, and I told him that I was born in Randers. He replied, in fluent Danish, that he himself had lived in Randers for six years, and when I asked him how that was possible, he told me the following story:

'When my father died, my uncle, who then lived in London, arranged that I could continue my schooling there. After passing my O-levels, I travelled around Europe during the summer vacation with the money I had saved working in my spare time. One day, I arrived in Copenhagen, and on talking to some foreign students was informed that I could apply to get an education in Denmark. I was lucky to get an apprenticeship in Randers.'

Abdi currently lives in Kenya. His sister, Fatuma, moved to Denmark after meeting her Danish husband while she was working as a nurse at a hospital in Saudi Arabia.

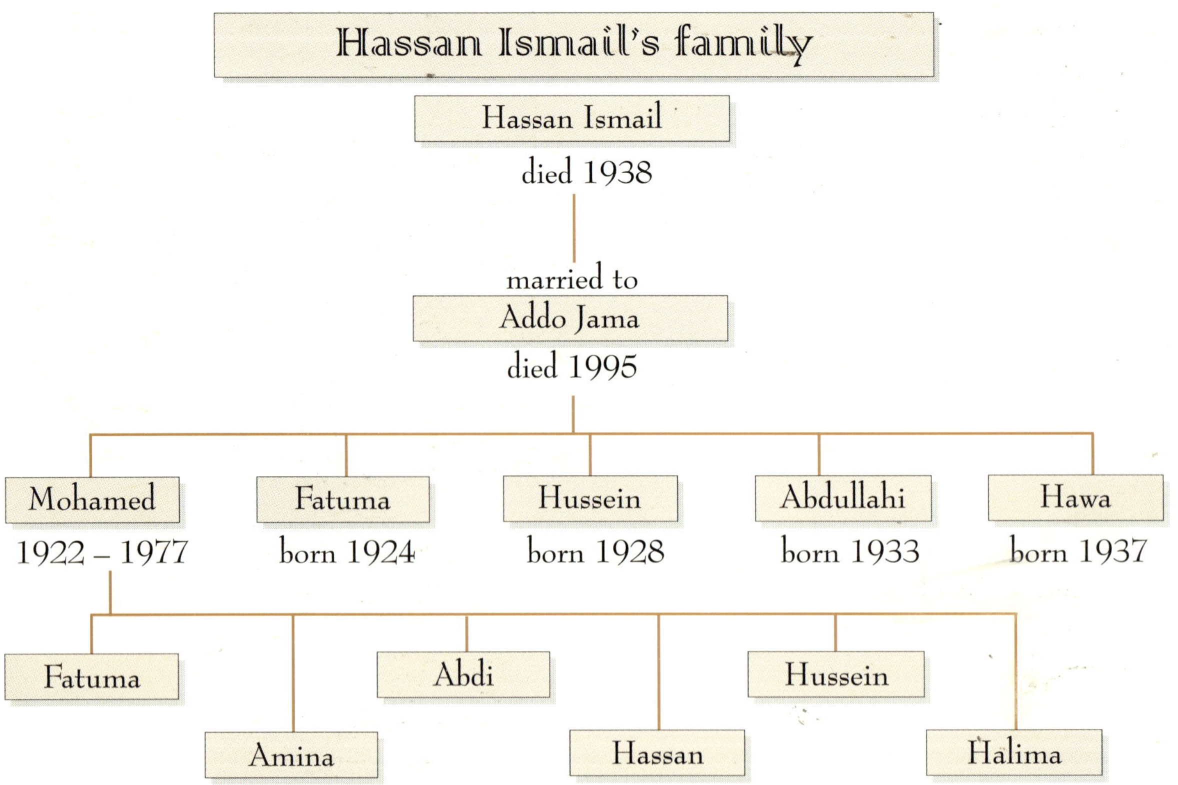

Nine

Juma bin Mohamed

Juma was employed at the Mbagathi farm in 1916 and moved with Karen Blixen to Mbogani the following year. He worked in the house until she left Kenya. Juma's father was Somali, like most of Karen Blixen's domestic workers, but his mother was Maasai.

Karen Blixen admired the Maasai and often mentioned them in her letters and books. They were her neighbours on the other side of the Mbagathi River, which divided her farm from their land, but they were often away as they took their cows wherever there was good grazing.

Juma is mentioned only a few times in Karen Blixen's letters. Once, when he had just been employed on the farm, Karen Blixen called him 'nice', but later she wrote that he sometimes behaved in a thoughtless manner.

Before Karen Blixen's mother was due to visit in 1924, Juma had been given three months' leave, so that he would be back when the guests arrived. During his leave, he gambled and lost everything he owned: money, cows and sheep. His poor family did not know where he was during that time, and when he finally returned to work, his ability to work was all that he had left to offer his family. In 1926, Karen Blixen

Juma bin Mohamed, circa 1932.

suspected that she could not trust him when she discovered some petty thefts in the house, including some shirt buttons that had disappeared.

'I don't think Juma is really responsible for his actions in such matters; he can do the most extraordinary things. Of course it *may* have been one of Denys' boys,—if not he himself,—who has taken them; but I have lost a number of things like this before and think everything indicates a house thief.'[88]

Karen Blixen was, however, very sympathetic towards Juma when he was ill with pneumonia in 1928. She had to take him to the hospital as his wives ('the beastly hags', as she called them), could not be bothered to send for her.

'Then he sent for me on Friday; he was certain he was going to die, and wanted to make a kind of will, which was chiefly to consist of his bequest of Tumbo to me. Tumbo came with me and is here now; he is so quiet and sorrowful, but the wives, heartless creatures, quite uncaring.'[90]

Juma survived both the suspicion of theft and his illness, and he stayed on at the farm as Karen Blixen's house help until she left Kenya. Maybe he owed this to his children, Mohu and Tumbo, for whom Karen Blixen had great fondness. She referred to them as

Juma bin Mohamed with his family. Tumbo, on the right, dressed in khanzu and fez. This photograph may have been taken on his first day of school.

'Tumbo is back at his school. I can't stop Juma's ambition for him, but he comes out here for weekends and then is made a great fuss over by the whole establishment, and actually I think he is quite happy "at Eaton", as Denys calls it.'[89]

her adoptive children, and they spent many hours in and around her house, away from their mother, who lived in the Somali village.

Juma's daughter, Mannehawa, born in 1918, was known to everyone as Mohuu. She helped Karen Blixen in the house and could lay a table and make toast when she was only four years old. Karen Blixen wrote to her mother that she had given her to Denys, who bought her shoes and a scarf. But she was also given clothes and presents by Karen Blixen, who found her to be brighter than European children of the same age.

Juma's son Mohamed, born in 1921, was for Karen Blixen the most irresistible of Juma's children. He was known as Tumbo, which in Kiswahili means stomach. Karen Blixen wrote about these children:

'It is Mahu's birthday today; she is five and is very excited about it. I have given her a necklace and a calf. She and her little brother who is two, have been romping around in here the whole morning while I have been writing, and holding a "Ngoma". The little boy, Tumbo, is the quaintest object, exactly like a frog, but he is afraid of nothing and roars with laughter and hits himself in the middle over all the eventualities of life.'[91]

Before her departure from Kenya, Karen Blixen wrote to her mother about Juma's plans for the future:

'Juma wants to go back into the Masai Reserve as a Masai, and so had to be re-registered as such. This we managed to do after some difficulty. He has acquired an excellent shamba out there and I promised him help in building himself a house, but it really is quite incredible how stupid the natives are. Of course I should have supervised the building a little and given him some advice, or found a proper fundee for him, but I took it for granted that he would be able to build a house for himself,—after all they build houses all the time and have done so for many thousands of years,—but I grew rather worried when I discovered how much timber,—which was what I had first promised him,—was going into it and found to my horror that he has built up the walls for a house 65 feet square. I really grew quite depressed as I sat there looking at it; I cannot imagine how they are going to get a roof on that house, and just the iron for it will cost 800 shillings, according to my calculations!— And I think it will collapse on top of them in the first gale. Juma could have been so comfortable if he had had a little common sense; but who would have thought he would be so crazy. Now I am going out there again today,—it is out near the Ngong,—with Farah and Juma and a fundee to look at it; I think they will just have to take the whole thing down again. I have promised Tumbo a cow, and my geese.'[92]

When Karen Blixen left Kenya, Mohuu was around 13 years old, but Juma was already busy arranging her marriage. Karen Blixen wrote in a letter that 'Mahaa is going to be married next year to a schoolteacher and I hope she will be happy with him.'[93]

Back in Denmark, Karen Blixen received a letter from Juma, in which he wrote about Mohuu's upcoming marriage:

'He also acquainted me with the negotiations around his daughter Mahô's marriage, speaking with scorn of the purchase-price offered by her Kikuyu suitor. The moving passage about my predilection for little Mahô and the trouble I had taken to teach her to read obviously called for a reply from me, which might prove useful in the bargaining.'[94]

Mohuu was married and had three children—one daughter and two sons. She lost her daughter some years back and died herself in a tragic accident in the early seventies, as a result of serious burns she sustained when her gas cooker exploded.

After Karen Blixen left the farm, Juma's family lived for many years in the house she had helped him to build, and he supported his family by working as a lorry driver. During the Mau Mau uprising in the fifties, the authorities wanted Juma to move, as the Kenyan freedom fighters had infiltrated the area where he lived. Juma refused, and he was finally arrested. His family was forced to move to a neighbouring farm.

Juma had twelve children, and he used the money he inherited from Karen Blixen in 1962 to pay for their education. He was at that time still working as a lorry driver in Kenya's Ministry of Agriculture but did not earn much from the job.

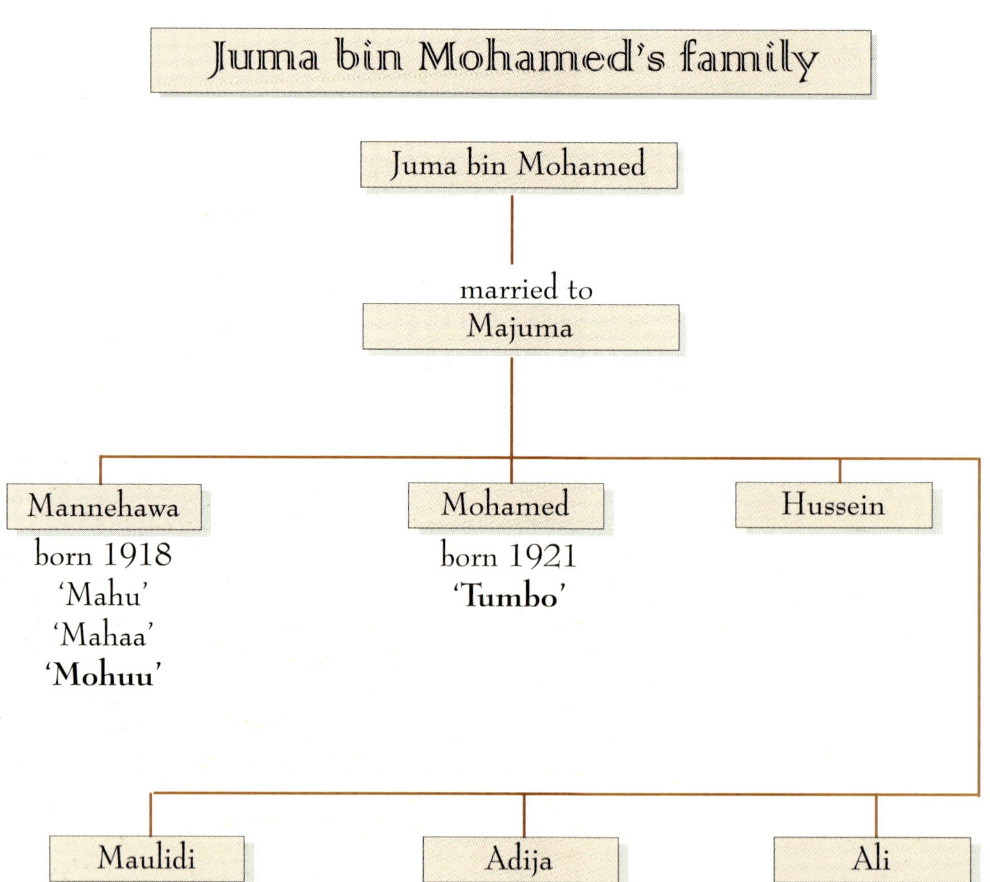

Ten

Mohamed bin Juma (Tumbo)

Tumbo lived with his mother in the Somali village some distance from the farm, but when he was about six years old, Karen Blixen talked Juma into letting him come to live on the farm. During the next few years, when he was not away at school, he would help Karen Blixen with small jobs like catching fish in the dam or looking after the dogs, which he still remembers as being very 'kali'.

Juma wanted Tumbo to go to school, and although Karen Blixen was not initially in favour of this, she eventually agreed to send him to a boarding school in Pumwani, a suburb on the northern outskirts of Nairobi. The reason for her reluctance was that she thought that the six-year-old Tumbo was too young to be away from home. When she took him to school on the first day, she 'bribed' the teachers to be nice to him. Today, Tumbo does not remember his first school in Pumwani, but he remembers that he had lessons in the school on the farm.

When Karen Blixen left Kenya, she had promised Tumbo a heifer and her geese as a farewell present, but he chose instead to accompany her on the train to Mombasa to see her off at the ship. It must have been a difficult choice for Tumbo, who had Maasai blood running in his veins, to choose to go

Mohamed bin Juma, 'Tumbo', circa 1928.

to Mombasa instead of owning a heifer. It suggests how fond he was of Karen Blixen, as the Maasai consider cattle to be the most important thing in the world.

Today, Mohamed lives in a big stone house in Bulbul Estate near the first house that Karen Blixen helped his father to build. The original house burned to the ground many years ago.

Mohamed bin Juma is now well into his seventies, but he is still in good health and very active, although his eyesight is not good. He is enjoying his retirement, together with his wife and those of his twelve children who are still living at home.

Asked about what he remembers best about Karen Blixen, Mohamed related a day on the farm when he was accompanying her on a walk with the dogs. She stopped and pointed across the coffee fields, and said to him: 'All those fields you can see from here, and much of the land which now belongs to European farmers will again one day in the future belong to your people.'[95]

To the young Tumbo this sounded like a fairy tale, and it was difficult for him to believe that what he heard could be the truth. He did not realize how far-sighted Karen Blixen was, and how many of her prophecies were to be fulfilled. Karen Blixen wrote

Mohamed bin Juma and his wife, Mishi Ngina, with some of their children, in 1963.

When Mohamed bin Juma was a little boy, Karen Blixen called him Tumbo, but he has long outgrown that name. He has lived most of his life in the same place, where he has become a well-known personality. It was, therefore, very easy to find his house in an area with no street names or house numbers. The house has a magnificent view to the Ngong Hills.

about Tumbo: 'Tumbo is such a sweet, frank and honest, friendly little person, and he seems to have a lot of friends at Pangani too, where he is probably the youngest boarder.'[96]

The same could be said for him today, except that he is no longer little, having grown into a tall, stately man.

Mohamed bin Juma will never forget Karen Blixen, and her book *Out of Africa* has an important place on the bookshelf in his house.

Tumbo and Sofe, two of Karen Blixen's African 'adoptive children', in 1931.

Sofe is wearing an amulet around his neck believed to protect him against all evil.

Sofe and Tumbo, in 1995.

It had been many years since these two childhood friends had last been photographed together. This photograph was taken outside Tumbo's house when they met again, in 1995. They had not seen each other much in the intervening years, except when they were brought together in Karen Blixen's name.

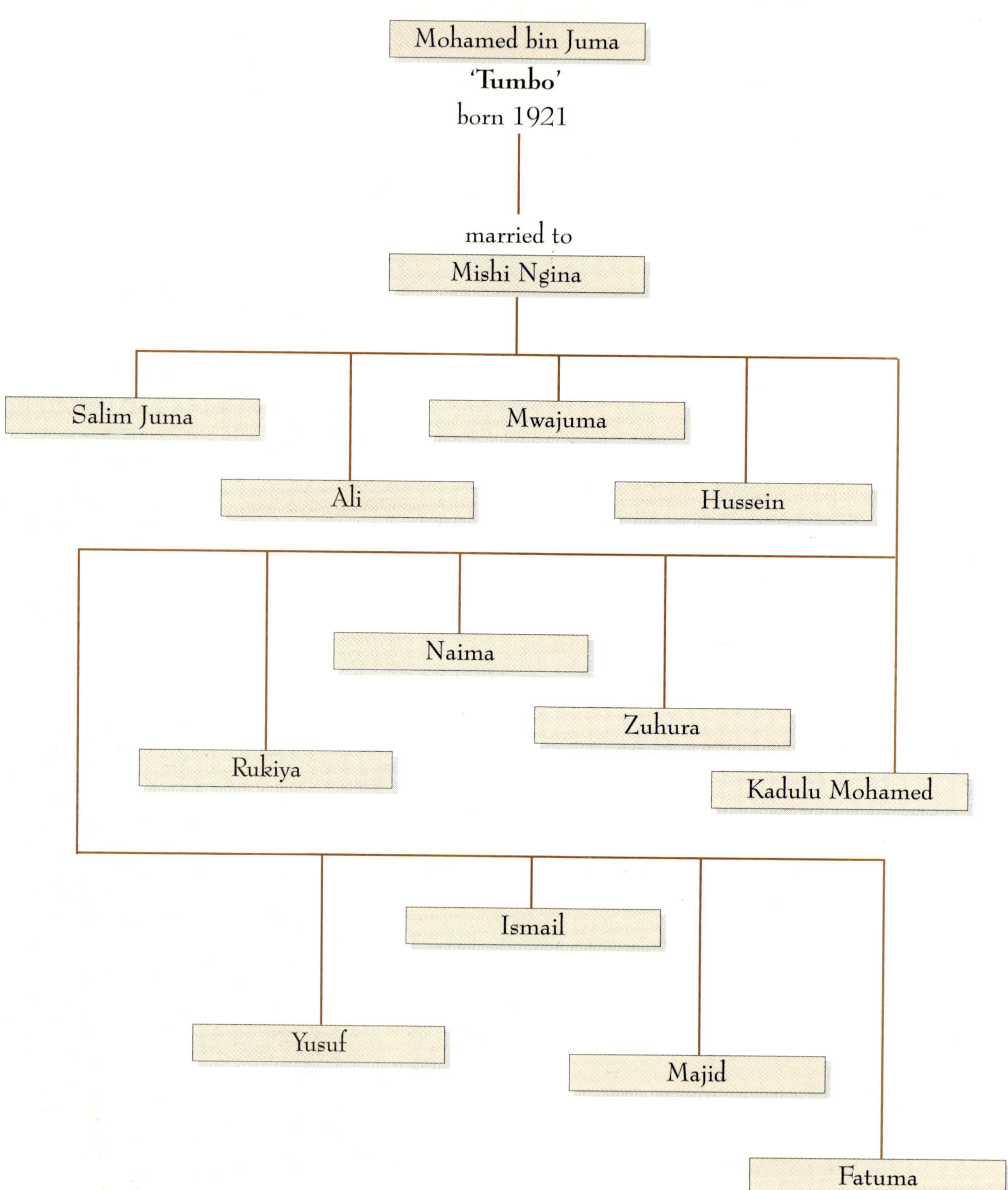
Mohamed bin Juma's family
Mohamed bin Juma
'Tumbo'
born 1921
married to
Mishi Ngina
Salim Juma
Ali
Mwajuma
Hussein
Naima
Zuhura
Rukiya
Kadulu Mohamed
Ismail
Yusuf
Majid
Fatuma

Eleven

Kamande wa Gatura

Kamande wa Gatura was born around the turn of this century, in Ndeya Village, in Kiambu District, central Kenya, where his father was a Kikuyu elder in Chief Kinanjui's council. Chief Kinanjui was a highly respected man, so when Kamande's brother Njuguna killed the chief's son Muthamba in a quarrel over a woman, Kamande and his family had to leave the village. It was purely by accident that they settled on Karen Blixen's farm. Kamande himself described how he met Karen Blixen one day on his way to the police station to report a man by the name of Oyamo for having stolen a chicken from him. Oyamo, who had promised to pay three rupees for the chicken, now suddenly refused to pay Kamande, who needed the money to pay the doctor to treat his bad leg. Karen Blixen, who spelled his name Kamante, described their first meeting from her point of view:

'I came upon him for the first time one day when I was riding across the plain of the farm, and he was herding his people's goats there. He was the most pitiful object that you could set eyes on. His head was big and his body terribly small and thin, the elbows and knees stood out like knots on a stick and both his legs were covered with deep running sores from the thigh to the heel.'[97]

Karen Blixen took pity on Kamande and, after an unsuccessful attempt to cure him herself, she sent him to the Scottish Mission Hospital where he stayed for three months, until he was completely cured.

Kamande wa Gatura, circa 1922.

When he came back to the farm, she employed him.

'Kamante, in all cooking matters, had a surprising manual adroitness. The greatest tricks and tours-de-force of the kitchen were child's play to his dark crooked hands; they knew on their own everything about omelettes, vol-au-vents, sauces, and mayonnaises. He had a special gift for making things light, as in the legend the infant Christ forms birds out of clay and tells them to fly.'[98]

When Karen Blixen left the country, Kamande was the employee she worried about the most, as she realized that life would be difficult for him in the future. She wrote:

'Kamante will of course lose his post and his shamba here, and despite his indisputable genius for cooking I am doubtful whether he will get another post; he is really rather lacking. But he is not so badly off; he has saved enough money here both to get married and to buy a couple of cows, so if only he finds somewhere to live,—like the other squatters,—he should be able to manage. He has two children of whom he is very fond. Titi is very miserable over my leaving; I think I shall give him a little bull that I have, to console him.'[100]

Karen Blixen was justified in her concern for Kamande's future. In 1931, he was a grown man with a wife and children, and

Kamande's brother Titi with Karen Blixen's dog, Sirius.

'Tell Tommy that I now have Kamante's little brother Titi as a dog toto,–I imagine Tommy can remember him. He has lost his job because Kamante sold all the goats and calves that he used to look after in order to buy his ndito; the other day when I was out for a walk with Heather and Titi he met some of his own calves in strange hands and burst into tears at the sight of them. This marriage has put Kamante so deeply into debt to me that I think he will have to be considered a slave for the rest of his life.'[99]

although he was employed occasionally by white settlers, they did not see in him the genius that Karen Blixen called 'caviar to the general'. 'Where the great Chef walked in deep thought, full of knowledge, nobody sees anything but a little bandy-legged Kikuyu, a dwarf with a flat, still face.'[101]

During the years that followed Karen Blixen's departure from Africa, she kept in contact with Kamande through letters and acquaintances who had met him.

'Kamante, however in this as in most other ways was different from the other people. As a correspondent he has a manner of his own. He puts three or four letters into the same envelope, and has them marked: *1st Letter, 2nd Letter*, and so on. They all contain the same thing, repeated over and over.'[102]

Karen Blixen gives an example of one such letter:

'I was not forget you Memsahib. Honoured Memsahib. Now all your servants they never glad because you was from the country, If we were bird we fly and see you. Then we turn. Then your old farm it was good place for cow small calf black people. Now they have no anything cows goat sheep they has no anything. Now all bad people they enjoy in their heart because your old servant they come poor people now. Now God know in his heart all this to help sometime your servant.'[103]

'Write and tell us if you turn. We think you turn. Because why? We think that you remembered still all our face and our mothers names.'[104]

She heard from others about Kamande's ups and downs, and she was sorry to hear that during the Mau Mau uprising in Kenya in the fifties, he had taken an oath, as had most Kikuyus, for which he was imprisoned for one year.

After Karen Blixen left Kenya, Kamande lived mostly on his family's farm in Kiambu, where all his troubles and the hard life probably contributed to his drinking too much. When the American photographer Peter Beard looked him up there in 1962, he was in almost as bad a condition as when Karen Blixen had met him on the plain for the first time. Peter Beard invited Kamande and his wife, Wambui, and all of his children to live at Hog Ranch, the farm he had bought in Langata, a suburb near the Mbogani farm. He built a house for them and gave Kamande a job as a watchman. He encouraged him to talk on tape about his life on the farm with the baroness, so that they could write a book together about it. During the next twelve years, Kamante talked about his life to a tape recorder, while some of his sons wrote his memoirs down on paper. During that time, Kamande and his sons also made some drawings, which they sold to make some extra money. Kamande also had a small part in the film *The Flame Trees of Thika*.

When the book *Longing for Darkness* was published in 1975, Kamande became famous again. The book did not make him a wealthy man, but it did result in a visit to England and Denmark, in 1975, where he had the opportunity to visit Karen Blixen's home in Rungstedlund, and lay flowers on 'his mother's grave'. While in Denmark, he was the guest of Thomas Dinesen, whom Kamande knew from his earlier visits to Kenya. Jacqueline Kennedy wrote the postscript in *Longing for Darkness,* and Kamande received a personal letter from her with a signed photograph.

Kamande's family, circa 1962. Back row, from right: Kamande's wife, Wambui, his brother Kiguru (Titi), his eldest son, Simon Gatura, his daughters Njoki and Wachura, and two grandchildren. Front row, from right: Kamande, his son Francis Kimani, Titi's son Gatura, and some of Kamande's grandchildren.

'Kamante was shrewd in money matters, he spent little, and did a number of wise deals with the other Kikuyu in goats, he married at an early age, and marriage in the Kikuyu world is an expensive undertaking. At the same time I have heard him philosophizing, soundly and originally, upon the worthlessness of money; he mastered it, but he had no high opinion of it.'[105]

Kamande disappeared again from the spotlight and lived quietly on Hog Ranch, his days interrupted only by visitors who came to see him, talk to him and obtain his autograph. Kamande was illiterate but he could write his name. Occasionally a photographer would ask him to pose for a picture to advertise various consumer goods.

During the seventies, some of those visitors appealed to the Danish Embassy in Nairobi for financial assistance to the aging Kamande. This resulted in a funds drive, which raised 17,000 Danish kroner for Kamande, a sizeable amount in those days. When invested, it gave Kamande a monthly income of about 300 kroner. Along with his salary as a watchman that he earned from Peter Beard, he was financially comfortable.

Kamande's dream, however, was to have his own house and a piece of land on which to

Kamande wa Gatura, Karen Blixen's cook in Africa, by the millstone table, in 1962.

'Kamante writes that he has been out of work for a long time. I was not surprised to hear of it, for he was really caviar to the general. I had educated a Royal Cook and left him in a new Colony. It was with him a case of "Open Sesame". Now the word has been lost, and the stone has closed for good round the mystic treasures that it had in it.'[106]

grow vegetables and keep a cow and a few sheep. He was convinced that his soul would never be able to rest in peace if he was not buried in his own soil. Until his death, Kamande supported several unemployed family members, and he wished to leave all his sons some kind of inheritance. After yet another fund-raising in Denmark and Kenya, Kamande finally got a small piece of land, a house and some livestock in Ongata Rongai, near the Ngong Hills, where it was the wish of the donors that he should live with his wife, Wambui, and his blind son, Mburu, for the rest of their lives.

Kamande died in July 1985 in his house on Peter Beard's ranch, where he was still living with Wambui and some of his children and grandchildren, but he was buried on his family's farm in Kiambu. Wambui has since died, but their grandson Moses still lives on Hog Ranch and looks after Kamande's house, which he has kept exactly as it was the day his grandfather died. The 'Danish' shamba in Ongata Rongai has been sold and the house moved to another family shamba, where the blind son, Mburu, now lives.

Kamande's own kitchen, in 1994.

In the house on Hog Ranch where Kamande died, everything has been preserved by his grandson Moses, who looks after his father's property. Kamande needed very few utensils to prepare a delicious meal.

'If Kamante had been born in Europe, and had fallen into the hands of a clever teacher, he might have become famous, and would have cut a droll figure in history. And out here in Africa he made himself a name, his attitude to his art was that of a master.'[107]

Much has been written and said about Kamande's financial situation, both in Kenya and in Denmark, and many people think that he was exploited and ought to have become richer by his involvement in films, interviews and the book *Longing for Darkness*. During the years that I knew Kamande personally, however, I never once heard him complain about his destiny. On the contrary, he always expressed his gratitude towards Karen Blixen and others for the help they had extended to him.

Kamande wa Gatura

Kamande's house on Hog Ranch, in 1994.

Kamande's grandson Moses, standing outside his father's house on Hog Ranch. He loved his grandfather and has baptized his own twin sons Kamande and Gatura. Kamande was the first of Karen Blixen's staff to be converted to Christianity. He was, therefore, one of the few who would handle a dead body, as most Africans at that time had serious aversions to this. Despite Karen Blixen's efforts, she was never able to talk him into attending her school.

'Kamante would then come with me, but he would not join the children on the school-benches, he would stand a little away from them, as if consciously closing his ears to the learning, and exulting in the simplicity of those who consented to be taken in, and to listen.' [108]

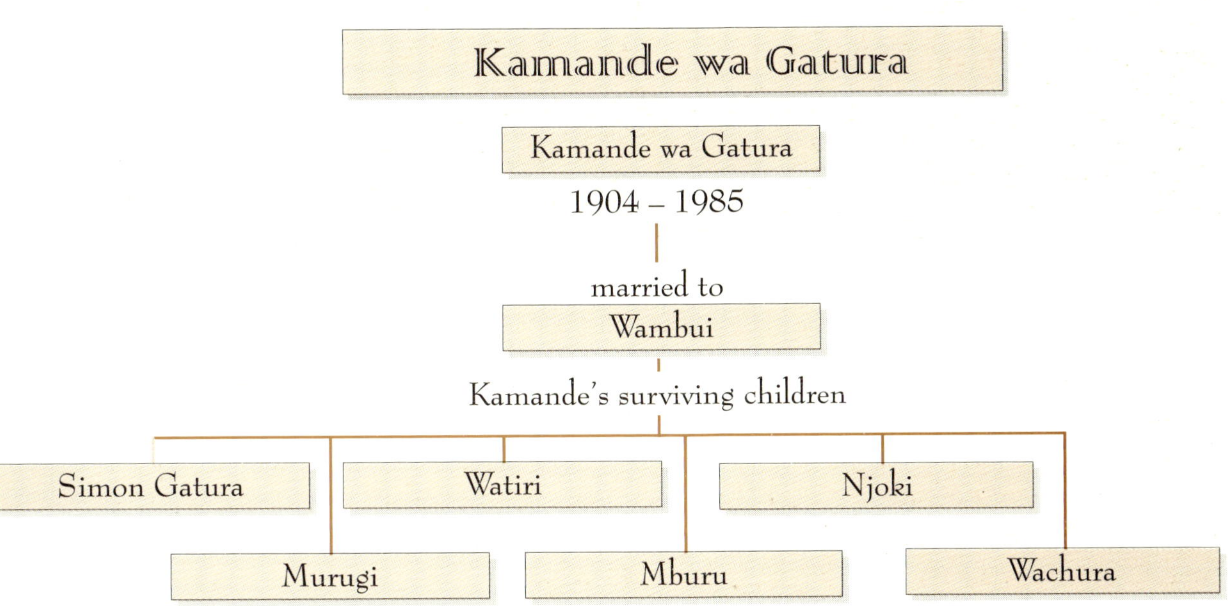

Twelve

Ali bin Hassan

Ali bin Hassan started his career with Karen Blixen on the first farm, Mbagathi, as a coffee picker, but when she moved to the much bigger house at Mbogani in 1917, he was promoted to work in the house. He would also accompany Karen Blixen on occasion when she went out to shoot to supply the farm workers with meat.

Ali was one of the many Somalis who worked in the house, but he was not mentioned in detail in her letters. It seems that she found his wife, Muara, whom he married in 1917, more interesting. Muara was very fond of the little motherless Halima and acted as her foster mother for a time. She once walked the long way to Nairobi, where Halima was staying at that time, just to catch a glimpse of her; but she did not dare speak to her for fear of making them both unhappy. When Farah's wife Fathima came to the farm in 1928, it was Muara who gave her lessons in Kiswahili.

When Karen Blixen left Kenya, she wrote to her mother about the plans she had made to secure Ali's future:

'Ali wanted to learn to drive a car and get his license before I left, so I have taught

Ali bin Hassan in his senior years.

him to drive and he got his license last Thursday. I don't think it will be difficult for him to find a job, although nothing is certain in these hard times. His father has a shamba in the Forest Reserve,—weren't we out there once?—and sounds well off. I intend to give Ali a cow as well.'[109]

After World War II, Karen Blixen lost contact with her African friends because Farah, her primary contact, had died. It was now left up to them to contact her.

'As to the others of my staff, now that I should no longer have Farah to look them up, it would, I reflected, be for them to find me. At the same time I could not be sure whether they would indeed set to do so or not. For they may not have grasped the fact that my long silence had been involuntary, but might quite well have taken it as a sign of my displeasure with them.'[110]

Destiny intervened in the form of one of Karen Blixen's friends. Sir Philip Mitchell, the British governor in Kenya, wrote to her that Ali was employed in his house and that he was the best worker he had ever had. Ali had asked him to write to her and explain that he would only stay and work for the governor until she herself returned to Kenya.

'I started on a correspondence with Ali. From the style of his letters I gathered that for these years he had—in contrast to earlier days—been living in a household with no financial worries. But he was faithful to the past, naming the horses and the dogs and bringing back things that I myself had forgotten.'[111]

An acquaintance of Karen Blixen's, Negley Farson, wrote about Ali in his book *Last Chance in Africa*:

'The Happy Valley lot has gone. With them has gone much of the reckless "Kenya way of life". They were lions among men, and the lions are going with them; I think they understood each other; both were unafraid. If you want to know what they were like, read Baroness Blixen's *Out of Africa*, one of the finest books ever to come out of that continent. I have lunched in the home that she lost and loved so much, with its dark paneled walls of wood brought out from Denmark; and I have met her boy Ali—still talking about her! He is now Governor Mitchell's majordomo on private train or safari or at the Thika fishing camp. Sir Philip told me that when he engaged Ali, that smiling boy said to him: "But remember, Bwana Makubwa, I am Memsahib Blixen's boy. If she comes back, I go to her!" I rose peak high in Ali's esteem when I told him I had lunched that charming woman in Copenhagen in November, 1939. I could do no wrong after that.'[112]

Ali also worked for a British farmer near Nakuru and then moved to Uganda, where he lived with his son for some years.

When Thomas Dinesen came to Kenya in 1964, to meet the five African heirs, he had not seen Ali bin Hassan and the other house staff since he had visited his sister in 1924. This historic meeting is described in the Danish newspaper *Berlingske Tidende,* 9 October 1964: 'Ali Hassan speaks English fluently, he bowed deeply, a little shy, but later the welcome became warmer and heartier, and he almost embraced Thomas Dinesen.'

Ali also told Poul Westphall of *Berlingske Tidende* how much Karen Blixen had meant to him and the other Africans on the farm:

Thomas Dinesen with some of the heirs, in 1964. From left: Sofe, Thomas Dinesen, Ali bin Hassan, Titi's son Gatura and Kamande. Karen Blixen's brother, Thomas, visited Kenya with his wife, Jonna, in 1964, to meet the five heirs. Farah's son Sofe and Juma's son Tumbo received the bequests on behalf of their fathers.

'She was a fine and noble human being, great with all her employees and good towards every needy person, we loved her and we cried like children the day she left the farm. The way in which she has thought about us during all these years, we have felt through the letters, which we exchanged, and now through this bequest, we have received from our good and loving genie.'[113]

Ali bin Hassan was at that time living on a small farm he had bought in Tanzania, and the money he received through Karen Blixen's will was used to build a proper house.

Thirteen

Farah Abedi

During my visit to Addo Hassan, her family members told me about a very old Somali gentleman by the name of Abedi, who lived in the neighbourhood. They knew that he had worked for Lord Delamere for many years and could tell stories about many of the famous European personalities who had lived in Kenya during the twenties, but they were not sure if he had known Karen Blixen.

I asked Sofe if he knew the old man, but he had not heard of him. A couple of weeks later, he called on me to tell me that he had found this mzee and asked him if he had known Karen Blixen. Sofe discovered that Abedi had not only known her but had worked on her farm for some years.

Sofe promised to arrange a meeting, and a few weeks later he came with Said, Abdullahi's son, to fetch me. Together we drove to Eastleigh to meet Abedi.

As we approached his house through a narrow street, a bus was parked in the middle of the road, apparently broken down, as it

Farah Abedi, in 1994.

Farah Abedi is today well over a hundred years old, but he still remembers Karen Blixen from the days when he worked on her farm. He was initially employed to look after Thomas Dinesen in the little house near Mbogani, but when Thomas Dinesen left, he became safari cook to Bror Blixen.

was surrounded by all its passengers. The only way to pass was between the bus and a street seller's stall, one in a row of many that lined the streets in front of the houses. A brisk trade in food, clothes and other essential goods was taking place there.

When we finally reached Abedi's house, a freshly painted, bright blue corrugated iron structure, Sofe went ahead to announce our arrival but came back to inform us that Abedi was having his bath. While we waited in the vehicle for what seemed hours, the temperature quickly rose, as the sun was beating down on the car roof without mercy. Outside it wasn't much cooler. It was a relief when we were at last summoned to the backyard, where a refreshed Abedi was waiting to receive us, seated under the flapping laundry. He told me that he was 109 years old, which made him exactly the same age Karen Blixen would have been had she still been alive. He appeared to be not only in good humour but also in great health. He was blind and hard of hearing, and he walked with some difficulty, but his memory had suffered nothing.

During the next hour, he told me that he had come to the Mbogani farm in the

Thomas Dinesen's house near Mbogani, circa 1922.

'I had him staying here again,–otherwise he has been living down at his bungalow near the factory,– but now he has gone back there again; he is very fond of having his own house, and it is in a beautiful situation. It is nice to be able to go down there for tea, it makes a pleasant change.'[114]

Thomas Dinesen lived for most of his three-year stay in Kenya in this beautiful bungalow. Today, the house has become an art gallery and is open to tourists, but it has undergone some alterations since Thomas Dinesen lived there.

early twenties and had worked in the small house where Thomas Dinesen stayed during his three-year visit.

'I cooked, washed and ironed and took care of all the work in the house. Bwana Thomas often had his meals together with his sister in her house, but when he ate in his own house he liked to have nyama choma, meat roasted over charcoal.'[115]

Abedi also told me that he occasionally went hunting with the baroness and Bwana Thomas, when he would carry the baroness's rifle, which he also loaded for her. Although he never worked in her house, he often came to the house to visit his friend Abdullahi.

When asked what he remembered about the baroness, he replied: 'She was a good and well-liked woman, always fair, even if she sometimes could get very angry, but her anger always disappeared as quickly as it occurred.'[116]

He would much rather talk about Bror Blixen, for whom he had worked as a safari

Bror Blixen on safari.

When Bror Blixen gave up life as a coffee farmer and moved from Mbogani in the early twenties, he supported himself as a professional hunter and safari leader. His cleverness as a hunter and talent for organization, together with good humour and irresistible charm, provided him with a natural and exciting livelihood. He was fortunate in enjoying robust health and indefatigable energy, as safari work is physically demanding. Although Bror Blixen earned a good income from his safaris, he never managed to save any money, because everything he earned was used in entertaining friends when he was back in Nairobi. Bror, who was a well-liked and very generous man, had many friends.

cook on several occasions. Abedi would never forget the two safaris he went on with Bror Blixen—first to Uganda with Sir Charles Markham and his new bride, Gwladys, and later to the Congo with Sir Charles as a client.

Bror Blixen stayed for a long time in the Ituri Forest in Uganda and became very ill at one point. He lost consciousness during an attack of malaria and was convinced that it was Abedi who saved his life.

'That evening I felt poorly myself. I had been out with Abedi to try and shoot something for the pot but hadn't seen anything and returned empty-handed. I told him to make up my bed and make a fire. I was cold and shivery and knew what was in store for me—fever and bed. I could see the dead men in front of me, sitting up in their graves, before the soil was shoveled in. When my bed was made I could hardly crawl to it. "Prepare a bath for me, Abedi," I said, "close to the fire and not too hot." When the bath was ready I took my temperature—102. I already felt confused. Again I saw the dead men, I heard weeping, and memories from my childhood came rushing back. Abedi helped me into the bath; my temperature had to be brought down. I took some aspirin and quinine and lost consciousness.

'I woke up in bed when Abedi tried to make me swallow a gulp of whisky. That swig is probably what saved my life. God, how weak I was and how difficult it was to breathe. My back ached, as did both my lungs. It was a bit easier when sitting up, so all we had in the way of cushions and blankets were put behind my back to prop me up. Abedi's girl was touching. She sat up all night, holding my hand, her black eyes wet with tears. I suppose she was thinking of the hour when she would help shuffle earth over me as I sat in the wet clay.'[117]

Bror Blixen took only two helpers with him on these safaris: Juma, the gunbearer, and Abedi, the safari cook. The two Somali men had befriended women in a village near their camp, and it was Abedi's girlfriend Suleima who stood vigil at Bror Blixen's sick-bed and held his hand throughout his illness. Abedi also recalled other exciting aspects of the safari and told me that they hunted the rare okapi and the white rhinoceros, which had been commissioned by the London Museum of Natural History.

When Bror Blixen no longer needed him, Abedi worked for Ake Bursell on his farm in Juja and was later employed by Lord Delamere and his wife, Gwladys, the former Mrs. Charles Markham, whom Abedi had met on safari with Bror Blixen. Abedi stayed on Lord Delamere's farm until he retired from work.

On our way back from Eastleigh, as we drove through the back streets of Nairobi, Sofe suddenly asked Said to stop the car outside a shop known as Kinanjui Motors. He disappeared into the interior of the shop and reappeared a few moments later somewhat disappointed. He told us that he had been in this shop one day looking for a spare part for his car and while talking to the owner had noticed a picture of Karen Blixen on the office wall. He was, of course, curious to discover how this picture had found its way there and was told that it had belonged to the owner's father, Chief Kinanjui, who had been a good friend of Karen Blixen's. Unfortunately, the owner of the shop was not in that day, and I missed out on a chance to hear yet another stanza of Africa's song of Karen Blixen.

Fourteen

Ngugi wa Thiong'o's Song

When the Danish Library Association celebrated its seventy-fifth anniversary in 1980, Kenyan author Ngugi wa Thiong'o was invited as a guest speaker. He opened his speech by quoting a Kenyan saying, which was printed in *Bogens Verden* of December 1980, as follows:

'We have a saying in Kenya that a person who rushes into a house where meat is being shared out is more likely to pick the innards. This is because he has not been in the house long enough to get used to the light and the shadows in the house or to familiarise himself with all the corners and with the faces of the people. He therefore tends to pick the first thing that comes his way. I feel slightly in that position today.'[118]

One has to assume that Ngugi wa Thiong'o was referring to the subject of the speech that followed, in which he claimed that Karen Blixen's book *Out of Africa* was one of the most dangerous books ever written about Africa. He felt that the racism portrayed in it, although camouflaged as love for the Africans, was the kind of love one has for animals, a claim he intended to prove by reading examples from it.

'When you have caught the rhythm of Africa, you find that it is the same in all her music. What I learned from the game of the country, was useful to me in my dealings with the Native People.'[119]

What she really meant, according to Ngugi, was that her knowledge of wild animals gave her the key to the African way of thinking.

'Kamante could have no idea as to how a dish of ours ought to taste, and he was, in spite of his conversion, and his connection with civilization, at the heart an errant Kikuyu, rooted in the traditions of his tribe and in his faith in them, as in the only way of living worthy of a human being. He did at times taste the food that he cooked, but then with a distrustful face, like a witch who takes a sip out of her cauldron. He stuck to the maize cobs of his fathers. Here even his intelligence sometimes failed him, and he came and offered me a Kikuyu delicacy —a roasted sweet potato or a lump of sheep's fat,—as even a civilized dog, that has lived for a long time with people, will place a bone on the floor before you, as a present.'[120]

Ngugi felt that Karen Blixen regarded Kamande as a civilized dog who had lived long together with white people, but he added in her defense that her racist attitude might be excused by the fact that she was a young romantic lady of the aristocracy when she wrote these lines. He felt, however, that the much older Karen Blixen ought to have thought more deeply when she wrote the following in *Shadows on the Grass*:

'The dark nations of Africa, strikingly precocious as young children, seemed to come to a standstill in their mental growth at different ages. The Kikuyu, Kawirondos and Wakamba, the people who worked for me on the farm, in early childhood were far ahead of white children of the same age, but they stopped quite suddenly at a stage corresponding to that of a European child of nine. The Somali had got further and had all the mentality of boys of our own race at the age of 13 to 17.'[121]

Else Brundbjerg refuted Ngugi wa Thiong'o's attack in *Bogens Verden* of October 1981. She is the author of the book *Kvinden, Kætteren, Kunstneren Karen Blixen* and has a very thorough knowledge of Karen Blixen's authorship, which she has studied for many years. The following extracts have been translated from Else Brundbjerg's reply to Ngugi.

'In an interview that followed his speech, Ngugi wa Thiong'o elaborated his opinions, and his speech and the interview are printed in *Bogens Verden*. [no. 10, 1980, and no. 1, 1981]

'Neither at the anniversary meeting or during the following interview were his allegations opposed in any way, so it must naturally follow that some of his misunderstandings are corrected. . . .

'The fundamental misunderstanding apparently arises because Ngugi wa Thiong'o assigns a meaning to the different words which does not correspond with Karen Blixen's, and he finds the proof of Karen Blixen's "undemocratic racism" in the fact that she compares Africans with animals in her books about Africa. This applies not only to Africans, though, as she also compares her very good English friend Berkeley Cole to a cat, and many similar examples can be found in her stories. It was part of her way of expressing herself. . . .'

'When she writes that what she learned in her association with wild animals could be used in her association with the native people, it is a quotation completely out of context. She also writes that the wild animals are shy and on guard and can move soundlessly and that you have to be careful not to frighten them. She felt that the same was applicable in getting to know the native people, as they would instantly retract to their own world. . . .

'Racism is, according to my dictionary, the belief in the superiority of a certain race. Karen Blixen did not think that the white race was superior in all areas, because she realised that civilization could divide the human being both from its own nature and from nature surrounding us, a view she held at a time when not many in the western world were aware of it. . . .

'In some ways the white race was superior; in other ways it was the black race. It was in the interaction between two different races that she saw a possibility for rediscovery, new discovery and development of ability in the human nature, irrespective of skin colour. . . .

'It is easy today to condemn colonialism in all its shapes. It is always easy to be wise after the event. We arrived with all our technical superiority, without thinking very much about destroying the African's culture and roots. Today, many have become wiser, and Karen Blixen's books about Africa, to say the least, can have added considerable significance to this understanding . . .

'Ngugi wa Thiong'o feels indignant that, in *Shadows on the Grass,* Karen Blixen writes about the Kikuyu as small children, as being far ahead of European children of the same age, but who then suddenly stop spiritually at a level comparable to a nine-year-old European child. I must admit that this can be misunderstood today, but it was maybe not totally inaccurate during the time she lived in Africa, when very few could read and write. . . .

'Her books about Africa are, in many ways, a contribution *for* the African's attitude to life and death, and they are, I suppose, first and foremost addressed to white people.'[122]

'I wish someone would explain this to Ngugi wa Thiong'o', says Else Brundbjerg at the end of her article.

Errol Trzebinski, who wrote *Silence Will Speak,* a biography of Denys Finch Hatton, also had comments on Ngugi wa Thiong'o's statements, when parts of his speech were reproduced in a Kenyan publication, *Viva Magazine,* March 1981. She claimed that his allegations about Karen Blixen's racism only exhibit his own racism, and that he lacked the ability to project himself back in time to enable him to understand other decades and to realize that people then had different sets of social mores, standards and values. Karen Blixen wrote about a time in Africa when schooling for Africans was almost nonexistent, and when Africans spoke only their own tribal language, not about today's Africa. Errol Trzebinsky ends her reply to Ngugi with a quotation from *Shadows on the Grass:*

'As here, after twenty-five years, I again take up episodes of my life in Africa, one figure, straight, candid, and very fine to look at, stands as doorkeeper to all of them: my Somali servant Farah Aden. Were any reader to object that I might choose a character of greater importance, I should answer him that that would not be possible.'[123]

Errol Trzebinsky then asks the reader if this is one of Karen Blixen's 'sickening views' or 'racism . . . persuasively put forward as love'—or if Ngugi will concede that it is a high tribute to a friend; a statement made with dignity and deep affection that has stood the test of time.

A Kenyan journalist, Wade Huie, asked Kamande during an interview printed in the *Standard* newspaper, on 21 August 1991, if Karen Blixen was a racist:

'The mzee did not hesitate for a second:

"That is a lie. Mrs. Karen was not a racist. She was Mzungu, but that didn't matter. Mrs. Karen had a very kind heart. She did not discriminate against African or Mzungu, child or grownup. There were very few quarrels because Mrs. Karen showed no tribalism; Kikuyu and Mkamba and Masai and Embu and even Muslims got along. She let us keep cows and have our own shambas, so nobody took the shamba to be European. It belonged to all of us. Everybody wanted to stay at Karen forever."'[124]

The manuscript left behind by Abdullahi Ahmed Weid after he died contains a chapter in which he describes Karen Blixen's attitude towards racism and the Africans who worked for her on the farm:

'Though there are very few people now living who knew Baroness Blixen, I am certain that every one of them would agree with me when I say that she did not believe in racial discrimination in any form. It would be no exaggeration to say that everyone who came in contact with her appeared to be an intimate friend. She had many friends among the Kikuyu community. They lived around her home. The Kikuyu women used to call her Njerri. I am told it means "a good Lady". The prominent Chief, Kinanjui, was really her great friend and she very often visited him at his home near the Kikuyu railway station.

'Karen Coffee Company owned two farms in the same area, both situated on the main road from Nairobi to Ngong. The smaller farm on the right side of the road was bought by the Baroness and her husband before I came from Somaliland. Both farms were planted with coffee and there were thousands of squatters, almost all of them Kikuyu. The Baroness used to visit them in their homes and chat with them freely in a friendly manner. She sometimes gave large parties for the Kikuyu women, literally inviting thousands. She entertained them in front of her house whenever it could not accommodate those invited. Kikuyu women would visit her just to see and talk to her. On many occasions I have heard the Kikuyu women telling the Baroness that she belonged to them. This was because they loved her.

'The Baroness felt that all were equal and that justice and fairness was everyone's right. In those days, racial discrimination in that multiracial country was similar to a war in which there was no actual field combat. The Baroness always pretended that racial discrimination was non-existent. She knew it existed but at the same time she knew she could do nothing to remedy the situation. She purposely avoided discussing it with anyone. Unlike the Europeans, the Baroness had many connections with the Somalis. She had a number of Somali domestic servants whom she treated more as friends than as servants. She also liked the Somali women very much. She attended almost every Somali wedding. The women called her "Utiyah" which means "of gentle outlook and soft feature". She often wore the dress of Somali women.

'Some Somalis were not friendly with the Somali servants of the Baroness. Although, honestly speaking, no one from the Somali community as a whole was displeased with the lady herself.

'I regard the baroness as "my mother by adoption", and can never forget her kindness to me. When I first arrived in Kenya at the age of 10, she employed me as a chokra, or sort of personal boy. Two years later she took the initiative in sending me to school in Mombasa. Later, for my personal convenience, she entered me in school in Nairobi. When she left for Europe in 1931, she left me a farewell gift of 200 shillings. In 1934 when I had established a petition-writing business in Bar in the former Somali Protectorate, she sent me a typewriter which was a great help to me in my business. After the success of her book, *Out of Africa,* in 1938, she sent me a thousand shillings thus allowing me a share in her success. She remembered me in her will in 1963, by leaving me the sum of five thousand Danish francs [kroner]. This was equivalent to 4000 shs. after tax deductions.

'It is for these many acts of kindness that I consider her my mother by adoption.'[125]

Fifteen

The Grave in Ngong Hills

One of the most important people in Karen Blixen's life in Africa was Denys Finch Hatton, her English friend, who died in a plane crash shortly before she left Kenya. She buried him in Ngong Hills, in accordance with a wish he once expressed when he and Karen Blixen went there on an excursion.

When you visit Karen Blixen's farm and sit at the millstone table, admiring the

Denys Finch Hatton, in 1931.

This picture was taken shortly before Denys Finch Hatton was killed in a plane crash at Voi, on 8 May 1931, and was sent to Karen Blixen after his death. Karen Blixen met Denys Finch Hatton at the Muthaiga Club, in Nairobi, in 1918, and they soon became friends. Their friendship developed into a relationship that Karen Blixen described in a letter to her brother, Thomas Dinesen, as follows: 'I believe that for all time and eternity I am bound to Denys, to love the ground he walks upon, to be happy beyond words when he is here, and to suffer worse than death many times when he leaves.'[126]

silhouette of the Ngong Hills, you feel an urge to see them up close. Karen Blixen had marked Denys Finch Hatton's grave so that she could see it from the millstone table, but that is no longer possible; you must go all the way to the hills to see it.

'I often drove out to Denys' grave. In a bee-line, it was not more than five miles from my house, but round by the road it was fifteen. The grave was a thousand feet higher up than my house, the air was different here, as clear as a glass of water; light sweet winds lifted your hair when you took off your hat; over the peaks of the hill, the clouds came wandering from the east, drew their live shadow over the wide undulating land, and were dissolved and disappeared over the Rift Valley.'[127]

'I bought at the dhuka a yard of white cloth which the Natives call *Americani,* and Farah and I raised three tall poles in the ground behind the grave, and nailed the cloth on to them, then from my house I could distinguish the exact spot of the grave, like a little white point in the green hill.'[128]

When I went in search of the grave myself for the first time, it was not as easy to find as I had believed; it was like trying to find a needle in a haystack. One day, after yet another failed attempt to locate the obelisk that marks the grave, I stopped the car and asked a group of school children if they knew where it was. They did, and they all offered to get into the car to show the way. This very lively crowd of guides obviously enjoyed this unexpected car ride and asked me to continue along the only road that runs parallel to the hills. Suddenly they all shouted that we had arrived. My glance followed the narrow, steep track up along a small square piece of land, and after a while I noticed the tall, grey stone obelisk, which Denys Finch Hatton's brother, Lord Winchilsea, had erected after the funeral. It was incredibly well camouflaged against a background of eucalyptus trees, whose trunks were all of exactly the same thickness and colour as the obelisk. Small wonder I had passed it so many times without seeing it. The grave was no longer located within the boundaries of the game reserve but on a farmer's small shamba, a coincidence that for many years made him very unhappy, as he often had tourist buses driving through his shamba, endangering the lives of his playing children and grazing livestock. Those who heard of his wish to get rid of the grave warned him that the ghost of Finch Hatton might then seek revenge.

By 1975, the grave was neglected and overgrown with weeds, and the original brass plaque with an inscription from Coleridge's poem 'The Ancient Mariner', long gone. I had read about the proud lions seen by the Maasai to be resting on the grave in the years following Denys Finch Hatton's death, but they had moved on in deference to civilization, and the only animals I saw on the grave were the farmer's peacefully grazing cows and goats.

The gravesite is easier to find today, as the owner of the farm has nailed a hand-painted signboard to the trunk of a tall cypress with the inscription 'D. Finch Hatton'. An arrow on the sign points the way to the obelisk. If you manage to take your car all the way up the rough track, you can park it on a small grassy patch, and from there follow the whitewashed line of stones marking the path through the maize field

Denys Finch Hatton's grave, Ngong Hills, in 1995.

In the field surrounding Denys Finch Hatton's grave, maize and potatoes are doing well in the fertile soil, and the grave itself has a beautiful flower bed. The fence on the right of the obelisk has been erected to prevent visitors from taking pictures without paying the entrance fee, and the old house in the background has been replaced by a newer and better one.

to the gate in the tall wooden fence, which has been erected to bar the view of the grave from the outside. Once you have paid to get inside, you are aptly rewarded, not only with the sight of the grave but also with a breathtaking panorama of the Athi Plains, with air as pure, clean and light, as Karen Blixen described it. A new brass plaque with the original inscription has replaced the missing one, and the playing children and the domestic animals have been moved to the upper half of the shamba, where a newer wooden house bears witness to new-found wealth.

Sixteen

Mbogani

The Africa Karen Blixen knew has long since disappeared, and very few of her young African friends from her days on the farm are still around today. The coffee trees have given way to a golf course, designed to attract buyers to the exclusive new housing estate, Karen, which emerged in the years following Karen Blixen's departure from Kenya; but the farmhouse that was her home for most of the 17 years she

The African farm seen from the east, in 1995.

'I have a large lawn in front of the house,–actually, on every side of it, as Njovana Bogani,–the Forest House,–is situated in the middle of a large forest, but I have not yet managed to get it mown by machine except in front of the house,–which is very popular with the totos who mind the goats; sometimes I have a hundred Kikuyu goats and sheep and a swarm of little brown youngsters in charge of them here, and with the delicate shadows of the trees on the grass I don't think there can have been anything lovelier to look at in Arcadia. Now and again they play the flute and dance; last Sunday they held a big dance for over a thousand people in front of my house.'[129]

The main street in Nairobi in 1914.

'It is impossible that a town will not play a part in your life, it does not even make much difference whether you have more good or bad things to say of it, it draws your mind to it, by a mental law of gravitation. The luminous haze on the sky above the town at night, which I could see from some places on my farm, set my thoughts going, and recalled the big cities of Europe. When I first came to Africa, there were no cars in the country, and we rode in to Nairobi, or drove in a cart with six mules to it, and stabled our animals in the stables of The Highland Transport.' [130]

lived in Africa is still there. It was originally built by a Swede, Aake Sjögren, who came to Kenya in 1911, on a big-game hunting safari with William Northrup McMillan. After the safari, the two men decided to invest in Kenya, and together they bought a big tract of indigenous forest 20 kilometres outside Nairobi, towards the Ngong Hills. They formed the Swedo-African Coffee Company, and started to clear 500 acres of the forest to make room for coffee trees. In 1911, Nairobi was the capital of Kenya but was by no means an impressive metropolis. Karen Blixen described it as follows:

'During all my time, Nairobi was a motley place, with some fine new stone buildings, and whole quarters of old corrugated iron shops, offices and bungalows, laid out with long rows of Eucalyptus trees along bare dusty streets. The Offices of the High Court, the Native affairs department, and the Veterinary Department were lousily housed, and I had a great respect for those Government Officials, who could get any work at all done in the little burning hot inky rooms in which they were set.

'All the same Nairobi was a town; here you could buy things, hear news, lunch or dine at the hotels and dance at the Club.'[131]

The Swedo-African Coffee Company was bought in 1917 by the Karen Coffee Company, Ltd., and Karen and Bror Blixen moved into the beautiful house in March of

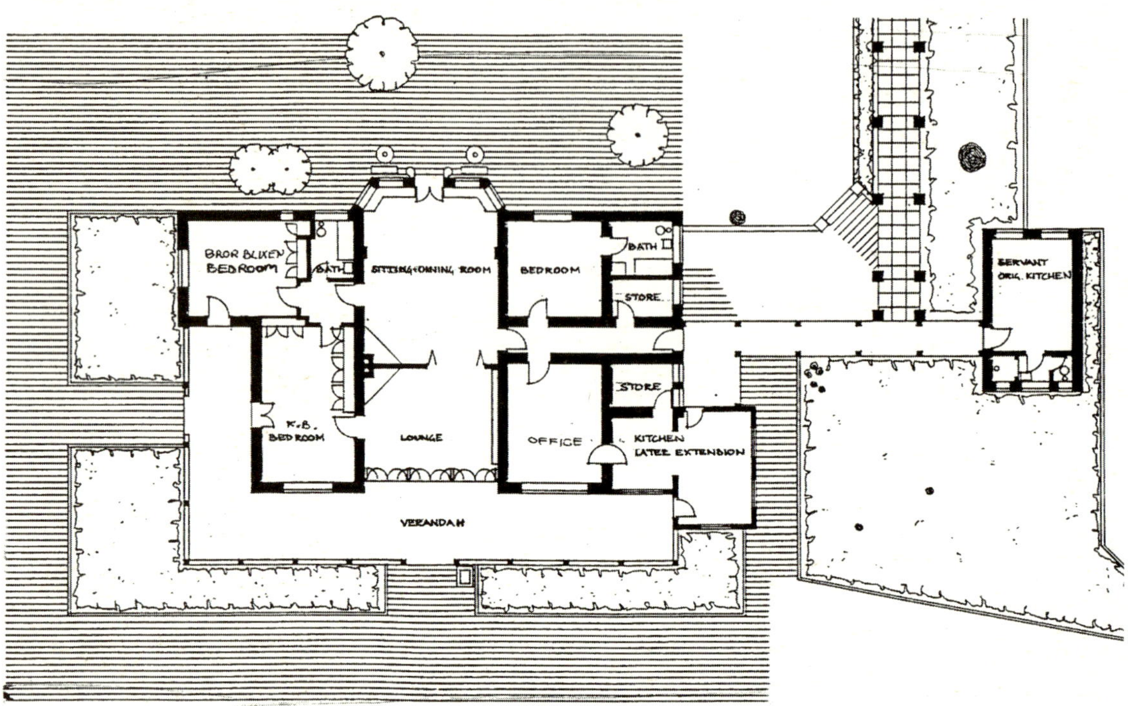

Plan of the Mbogani house as it looks today.

Few changes have taken place in the house since Karen Blixen left it. The veranda extended in those days around the house on the north side but was later to become part of a modern kitchen. Today, it is the Museum shop. The original outdoor kitchen has also been renovated and made to look as it would have when Karen Blixen lived there.

that year. The house was built on a flat area to Aake Sjögren's own design and has remained almost unchanged until today. It is a well-built house and the materials used were the best available in Kenya at that time. It was built in natural grey stone, surrounded by a wide veranda, which shades it from the sun on three sides, keeping the temperatures inside pleasant.

The largest room in the house, with its lofty ceiling, dark cross-beams and wooden paneling made from Kenyan Mvuli, was used by Karen Blixen as a dining room. In one corner, adjoining the sitting room, is a stone-built corner fireplace, over which a section of the wooden paneling is decorated with a beautiful linen-fold design. Another room, which the Blixens used as their office, also has wooden paneling.

The sitting room is separated from the dining room by a wide wooden folding door, and it was in this room, in front of the other corner fireplace, that Karen Blixen entertained her guests with stories, many of which were inspired by the French hand-painted screen. One wall in this room is completely covered by a bookcase, which was specially designed for Denys Finch Hatton's book

Karen Blixen's sitting room at Mbogani, in 1985.

In this room are the book cases that Karen Blixen had made for Denys Finch Hatton's extensive book collection. Karen Blixen entertained her guests here after dinner while classical music played on the gramophone, a gift from Denys Finch Hatton. The French hand-painted screen, reconstructed with photographs of each of the panels on the original screen, was placed in front of the door to Karen Blixen's bedroom and was often used to inspire the stories she told to her guests. Sometimes it would seem like the figures on the screen came to life in the flickering light from the fireplace. The original screen is at Rungstedlund, Karen Blixen's home in Denmark.

collection. After his death, Karen Blixen put two small brass plates with the initials 'DFH' on it. The beautiful wooden floors in these two rooms are made from local cedar wood.

There are three bedrooms in the house and two bathrooms. The one bathroom that was shared by Karen and Bror Blixen had a door leading outside, which was used by the staff when they carried the bath water to or from the house. The other bathroom is adjacent to the guest bedroom.

The kitchen, which in those days was always outside the house because of the open fireplace and the risk of fire, was connected to the house by a covered passage. There was no electricity and no running water when they moved in, and food was cooked on a dover-stove. It was common practice in the early days in Kenya to keep the fire in the stove going all day by pushing forward a big branch or piece of wood as it burned. One of Aake Sjögren's first houseguests at

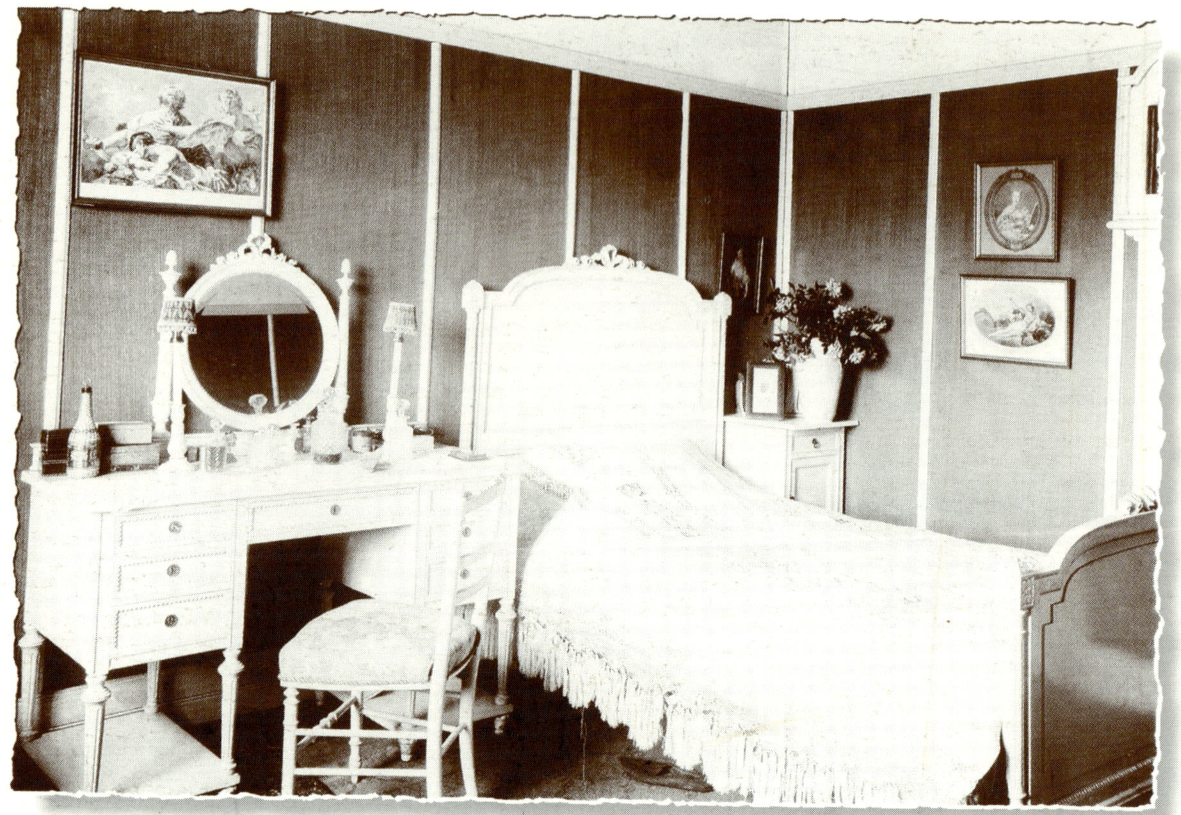

Karen Blixen's bedroom at Mbagathi, in 1914.

'All the inside walls of the house are wooden, but Bror had had them very well done up, covered with canvas part of the way up (to the upper lintel of the doors, as a sort of paneling): this is topped by a broad wooden list, and above that they are white, nice and fresh looking. In here in my bedroom it is pale grey which goes well with my pink rugs and flowered cretonne.'[132]

Swedo, as he called the farm, was Prince Wilhelm of Sweden, who used the house as his headquarters during his safaris in Africa. Since that time, many famous and interesting people have crossed its threshold, as Karen Blixen opened her doors to a mixture of visitors, among them an Indian High Priest, titled Europeans, her staff and their families, African chiefs and poor countrymen. She loved to entertain guests, and it was always a happy occasion when her friends arrived; she called them'heavenly messengers'. In 1928, the Prince of Wales came for dinner.

Karen Blixen first thought of naming the house 'Frydenlund', or 'Fuglsang', but as nobody could pronounce these names, and the Africans already referred to the farm as 'Mbogani', which in Kiswahili means 'in the forest', she decided to call it just that. Today, the forest is gone and only a few of the original trees remain.

Karen Blixen lived at Mbogani until she left Kenya, in 1931. The farm was sold to an estate agent, and the house remained empty until it was rented, in 1933. In 1935, it was sold to a retired English colonel from India, who had come to live in Kenya with

Karen Blixen's bedroom at Mbogani, in 1985. The bedroom has been restored according to a photograph Karen Blixen sent to her family in Denmark and can be seen at the Karen Blixen Museum, in Nairobi.

When Karen Blixen moved to Mbogani in 1917, the new house was fully furnished, but she brought with her some of her old furniture from Mbagathi, including the bedroom furniture pictured here. When she was unwell and bedridden, it was important for her that the bedroom was pleasantly furnished.

'But just at present I am not very well: I think I have a touch of sunstroke and I am making use of the time while Bror is in Mombasa to stay in bed. My boys are so exceptionally good, and in this lovely cool clean house it is a real pleasure, almost like the National Hospital.'[133]

his wife and two daughters. He was so taken with the house, in its beautiful surroundings, that he bought it together with 36 acres of surrounding land. He lived there until his death in 1954. His wife laid out the garden and planted the large cactus bed in front of the house. When Karen Blixen lived on the farm, the house was surrounded mostly by nature. After the death of the colonel, one of his daughters lived in the house with her family for a while, until it was again offered for sale in the late fifties.

The house was then vacant until it was bought by the Danish government with the intent of presenting it to the new Kenyan government on the occasion of independence celebrations on 12 December 1963. Together with the house and 36 acres of land,

Mbogani seen from the west side, in 1985.

Karen Blixen often sat on this side of the house and enjoyed the view of the Ngong Hills, which lie to the southwest of the farm.

'The hills from the farm changed their character many times in the course of the day, and sometimes looked quite close, and at other times very far away. In the evening, when it was getting dark, it would first look, as you gazed at them, as if in the sky a thin silver line was drawn all along the silhouette of the dark mountain; then, as night fell, the four peaks seemed to be flattened and smoothened out, as if the mountain was stretching and spreading itself.' [134]

the gift also included the establishment of a domestic science college for women to be built on the grounds, with enough funds to run it for five years while Kenyan staff was being trained. Karen College, as it was called, opened on 9 September 1966, and the farmhouse became the residence of the college matron. In 1985, it became the Karen Blixen Museum.

Many Danes have dreamt of restoring Karen Blixen's famous farm and turning it into a museum, so that Karen Blixen admirers may see for themselves how she lived. After the release of the film *Out of Africa*, interest in Kenya and Karen Blixen was renewed, and the Kenyan government and the National Museums of Kenya finally approved the project.

It was intended from the beginning that the museum should attempt to give visitors an impression of how Karen Blixen lived in Africa, as well as portray the lives of the early settlers. At the same time, visitors to the museum would learn about the history of coffee-growing in Kenya, and the development of agriculture through the ages by looking at pictures and exhibits. The setting should, of course, be the farmhouse, with as much original furniture as was possible to collect, arranged in the same way as shown in Karen Blixen's photographs.

It was challenging to try to reconstruct details in the old house. The dark wood paneling was covered with many layers of yellow plastic paint. By carefully scraping off old paint, it was not only the old paneling that surfaced but also the original colours in the rest of the house. Universal Pictures, when preparing to film *Out of Africa*, sent their experts to scout for any original furniture still remaining in Kenya and after completion of the film, generously donated many pieces to the Karen Blixen Museum, along with other objects similar to the ones Karen Blixen had when she lived there. Her family in Denmark donated a painting and a porcelain figurine of a turkey that Karen Blixen had with her in Kenya. The famous bust of Karen Blixen sculpted by Harald Isenstein was copied and donated to the museum by Isenstein's heirs. A tea set similar to the one Karen Blixen brought to Kenya and two Royal Porcelain figurines of Harlequin and Columbine were presented to the museum by the Royal Porcelain Factory in Copenhagen. A committee of interested people in Denmark, headed by Else Brundbjerg, had copies made of Karen Blixen's African paintings, which were photographed by Vavara Hassalbalch and then laminated onto canvas. This process so closely replicated the original paintings that many visitors to the museum think they are seeing originals. The Danish committee ensured that photographs of the rooms in the house as they were furnished by Karen Blixen when she lived in them were made available to the Kenyan museum. It also raised a substantial amount of money in Denmark for the Kenyan project.

When Karen Blixen was packing her furniture in preparation for her departure from Kenya, she received an invitation to the opening of the McMillan Memorial Library, built by Lady McMillan in the centre of Nairobi, in memory of her late husband, Sir Northrup McMillan. Karen Blixen, a good friend of Lady McMillan, sold her many pieces of furniture that she did not wish to ship back to Denmark. These can still be seen today at the McMillan Memorial Library.

During the renovations of the Karen Blixen Museum, I spent many hours in the house. When you sit with your eyes closed in one of the quiet rooms, you can feel its special atmosphere. There is a light, fleeting, indefinable fragrance that emanates from the dark panels. Maybe it is the fragrance of the past, from the time when Karen Blixen lived in these rooms. From the stone bench by the millstone table in front of the house, the Ngong Hills form the same backcloth on the western horizon as when Karen Blixen watched them; the enchanting cloud formations above the hilltops are still constantly changing .

The Karen Blixen Museum is one of the most popular tourist attractions in Kenya today, with safari buses bringing tourists from all over the world to see it. The museum facilities can be rented for occasions such as concerts, memorial services, weddings and other special events. On the lawn in front of the house, where the big ngomas were held throughout the night in Karen Blixen's time, and where the proud warriors once danced their traditional dances, one can now see modern brides and men in western suits; the African drums, which could be heard far into the moonlit nights, have been replaced by modern rhythms.

Golf is today played on the old coffee fields, and if you care to listen to the old Africans in the area, they will tell you that Karen Blixen's school used to be where now lies the sixteenth tee, and that the exciting lion hunt, when two lions were shot in the coffee field near the house, took place on the fourth fairway. They will also show you where Denys Finch Hatton landed his plane on the farm, today called Ndege Road, which in Kiswahili means 'the road of the bird'.

Seventeen

Last Song

'Does Africa know a song of me?', asked Karen Blixen.

Yes, Africa knows a song of Karen Blixen, and even if many years have passed since she left the farm in Kenya, the song can be heard stronger today than ever before. But the Africa that Karen Blixen knew, and knew a song of, has long gone, and big changes have taken place in the intervening years. The magnificent landscapes, the wild animals and the dazzling white beaches on the Indian Ocean have always enticed tourists to Kenya and are still the greatest attractions, but many come today also to stand in Karen Blixen's footprints. They want to see the farm where the famous author lived as well as Denys Finch Hatton's grave in the Ngong Hills, and the names of the two are therefore often used as bait in tourist brochures. A safari camp has been named Finch Hatton's Camp, and although Karen Blixen has not yet lent her name to a hotel, 'Out of Africa' has become a household name and is widely used to promote consumer goods. Karen Blixen's name is still known all over Kenya, and the song of her life in Africa will be heard far into the future.

Since coming to Kenya, I have collected material for my scrapbook about Karen Blixen and her life in Africa. As the number of pages grew and I came into contact with the many people whose lives have been touched by Karen Blixen, I felt that the figures mentioned in her books and letters started to come alive. I was intrigued to discover that the same thing had happened to some of the people I interviewed—those who in some way were connected to Karen Blixen's life on the farm. In the beginning, many simply answered my questions, but later on, I sensed an increased interest in the person, Karen Blixen, and when they realized that it was also their own past they were researching, and that they were themselves part of the history they were revealing, they often took the initiative to research further.

Before I finish my song about Karen Blixen, it is important to me to thank the people who have helped me in different ways to put this book together.

There are three people I especially want to thank, because without them I could not have written the book. Two of them live in Kenya: Farah's son, Sofe, and Abdullahi's son, Said, whose hard work and enthusiasm enabled me to locate many of the key people in this book. Their support and inspiration have been indispensable. The third person to whom I am indebted is Else Brundbjerg, who with her thorough knowledge of Karen Blixen, her life and authorship, has helped me to weed out mistakes and misunderstandings. Kamande, Addo Hassan and Farah Abedi, who knew Karen Blixen and who had themselves experienced colonial life in the beginning of this century; Farah's children, Ali and Asha; Juma's son, Tumbo; Kamande's grandson, Moses; as well as Hassan Ismail's grandchildren, Abdi and Fatuma, have all given me glimpses of family members and thereby helped to illuminate the profiles of the people mentioned in this book.

A special thank you goes to Clara Selborn for her help and support, and to Hans Berggreen of the Karen Blixen Archives at the Royal Library, Copenhagen, for guiding me through the African section of photographs in the archives; my two daughters, Jamila and Tanya Karima, for their relentless critique; my husband, Akbar, for his help with the photographs and his encouragement; and my friend Jolene Wood for proofreading. I am also indebted to Helen van Houten and Damary Odanga for their work in editing, formatting and typesetting the book.

There are, of course, many others to whom I owe thanks for assistance and support, but it would be too extensive to mention everyone here by name.

Notes

The following abbreviations have been used when referring to the major publications:

FARAH Karen Blixen, *Farah. Radioen den 24 marts 1950* (Wivels Forlag, Copenhagen, 1959).
LCIA Negley Farson, *Last Chance in Africa* (Victor Gollancz Ltd., London, 1950).
LFA Karen Blixen, *Letters from Africa 1914–31*, edited by Frans Lasson (Pan Books Ltd., London, 1986).
OOA Isak Dinesen, *Out of Africa* (Random House, New York, 1938).
SOTG Isak Dinesen, *Shadows on the Grass* (Michael Joseph Ltd., London,1961).
TAL Bror Blixen, *The Africa Letters,* edited and with an introduction by G.F.V. Kleen (St. Martins Press, New York, 1988).
THOA John Buchholzer, *The Horn of Africa* (Adventurers Book Club, London, 1959).

1. OOA: p. 79.
2. OOA: p. 7.
3. OOA: p. 4.
4. OOA: p. 17.
5. SOTG: p. 10.
6. LFA 1914–31: p. 409.
7. LFA 1914–31: Introduction to the first letter.
8. LFA 1914–31: p. 18.
9. LFA 1914–31: p. 3.
10. LFA 1914–31: p. 45.
11. LFA 1925–31: p. 407.
12. OOA: p. 8.
13. LFA 1914–31: p. 7.
14. OOA: p. 7.
15. OOA: p. 7.
16. OOA: p. 3.
17. SOTG: p. 12.
18 OOA: p. 158.
19. OOA: p. 144.
20. LFA 1914–31: p. 285.
21. Interview with Kamande wa Gatura 1975.
22. LFA 1914–31: p. 132.
23. LFA 1914–31: p. 310.
24. LFA 1914–31: p. 363.
25. LFA 1914–31: p. 407.
26. OOA: p. 179.
27. SOTG: p. 86.
28. SOTG: p. 86.
29. SOTG: p. 86.
30. SOTG: p. 86.
31. SOTG: p. 97.
32. THOA: p. 31.
33. THOA: p. 31.
34. SOTG: p. 21.
35. LFA 1914–31: p. 1.
36. LFA 1914–31: p. 4.
37. SOTG: p. 21.
38. FARAH: p. 21.
39. LFA 1914–31: p. 416.
40. LFA 1914–31: p. 31.
41. LFA 1914–31: p. 39.
42. LFA 1914–31: p. 43.
43. LFA 1914–31: p. 54.
44. LFA 1914–31: p. 417.
45. LFA 1914–31: p. 275.
46. SOTG: p. 21.
47. LFA 1914–31: p. 330.
48. LFA 1914–31: p. 431.
49. SOTG: p. 23.
50. LFA 1914–31: p. 42.
51. LFA 1914–31: p. 289.
52. SOTG: p. 9.
53. LFA 1914–31: p. 23.
54. LFA 1914–31: p. 71.

55. LFA 1914–31: p. 334.
56. OOA: p. 175.
57. OOA: p. 185.
58. OOA: p. 186.
59. OOA: p. 182.
60. SOTG: p. 87.
61. OOA: p. 110.
62. OOA: p. 13.
63. LFA 1914–31: p. 405.
64. Interview with Kamande wa Gatura 1975.
65. LFA 1914–31: p. 1.
66. OOA: p. 101.
67. SOTG: p. 9.
68. LFA 1914–31: p. 423.
69. OOA: p. 386.
70. SOTG: p. 40.
71. LFA 1914–31: p. 415.
72. LFA 1914–31: p. 417.
73. LFA 1914–31: p. 414.
74. SOTG: p. 29.
75. SOTG: p. 14.
76. OOA: p. 183.
77. Abdullahi's manuscript.
78. SOTG: p. 88.
79. LFA 1914–31: p. 152.
80. Abdullahi's manuscript.
81. SOTG: p. 87.
82. LFA 1914–31: p. 273.
83. SOTG: p. 92.
84. SOTG: p. 91.
85. LFA 1914–31: p. 74.
86. Interview with Addo Hassan Juli 1993.
87. Interview with Addo Hassan Juli 1993.
88. LFA 1914–31: p. 239.
89. LFA 1914–31: p. 319.
90. LFA 1914–31: p. 379.
91. LFA 1914–31: p. 175.
92. LFA 1914–31: p. 424.
93. LFA 1914–31: p. 425.
94. SOTG: p. 86.
95. Interview with Mohamed bin Juma, January 1995.
96. LFA 1914–31: p. 319.
97. OOA: p. 22.
98. OOA: p. 37.
99. LFA 1914–31: p. 334.
100. LFA 1914–31: p. 424.
101. OOA: p. 81.
102. OOA: p. 80.
103. OOA: p. 81.
104. OOA: p. 81.
105. OOA: p. 33.
106. OOA: p. 80.
107. OOA: p. 36.
108. OOA: p. 32.
109. LFA 1914–31: p. 424.
110. SOTG: p. 97.
111. SOTG: p. 97.
112. LCIA: p. 64.
113. Berlingske Tidende, October 1994.
114. LFA 1914–31: p. 121.
115. Interview with Farah Abedi, October 1994.
116. Interview with Farah Abedi, October 1994.
117. TAL: p. 122.
118. Bogens Verden, December 1980.
119. OOA: p. 16.
120. OOA: p. 38.
121. SOTG: p. 15.
122. Bogens Verden, 9 October 1991.
123. SOTG: p. 9.
124. East African Standard 21 August 1991.
125. Abdullahi's manuscript.
126. LFA: 1914–31: p. 224.
127. OOA: p. 358.
128 OOA: p. 358
129. LFA: 1914–31: p. 54.
130. OOA: p. 10.
131. OOA: p. 11.
132. LFA 1914–31: p. 7.
133. LFA 1914–31: p. 48.
134. OOA: p. 5.

Glossary

americani	an unbleached calico cloth
asante	thank you
askari	soldier
bakshishi	gratuity, gift, tip (also bukshishi)
barua	letter
Bwana	Mr., sir
chokra	personal servant
choma	burn, roast
duka	shop, stall (also dhuka)
dukawallah	shop owner
Embu	Kenyan tribe
fez	cylindrical red hat with tassel, worn by many Muslims
fundi	skilled craftsman (also fundee)
jembe	hoe
kakele	*see* kelele
kali	sharp, angry, fierce
kanzu	long-sleeved white outer garment worn by men, reaching from the neck to the ankles
Kawirondo	Kenyan tribe
kelele	noise, shouting
khanzu	*see* kanzu
Ki-Swahili	Bantu language, mixed with Arabic, spoken by most Kenyans
kidogo	small
Kikuyu	Kenyan tribe
Maasai	Kenyan tribe
Memsab	Mrs., Madam (also Memsahib)
Meru	Kenyan tribe
Mkamba	Kenyan tribe
mkubwa	big, wide, high, superior
mlango	door, gate
mzee	old man; a respectful title
mzungu	European
ndito	young unmarried woman
ngoma	dance, drum
nyama	meat
nyama choma	roast meat
Poor Box	Karen Blixen's horse
rupee	Kenyan coin
safari	travel
salaam	peace; a greeting
sana	very much
shamba	farm, field, garden, plantation
shauri	problem
squatter	a person living on another person's property with no legal authority
toto	child
tribalist	a person with strong, often biased ethnic feeling
tumbo	stomach

Bibliography

Abokor, Axmed Cali. *The Camel in Somali Oral Traditions*. Motala Grafiska, Motala, Sweden, 1987.

Beard, Peter. *Longing for Darkness—Kamante's Tales from Out of Africa*. Sidney Rapoport, U.S.A., 1975. N.Y.

Blixen, Bror. *The Africa Letters*. Edited and with an introduction by G.F.V. Kleen. St. Martin's Press, New York, 1988.

Blixen, Karen. *Letters from Africa 1914–31*. Edited by Frans Lasson. Pan Books Ltd., London, 1986.

———. *Farah. Radioen den 24 marts 1950*. Wivels Forlag, Copenhagen, 1959.

———. *Farah*. Nordlunde, Copenhagen, 1950.

Buchholzer, John. *The Horn of Africa*. Adventurers Book Club, London, 1959.

Christensen, Helge. *Juma og Kamante*. J. H. Schultz A-S, Universitets Bogtrykkeri, Denmark, 1950.

Dinesen, Isak. *Out of Africa*. Random House, New York, 1938.

Dinesen, Isak. *Shadows on the Grass*. Michael Joseph Ltd., London, 1961.

Dinesen, Thomas. *Safari Dagbog*. Gyldendal, Copenhagen,1982.

Farson, Negley. *Last Chance in Africa*. Victor Gollancz Ltd., London, 1950.

Huxley, Elspeth. *Settlers of Kenya*. Greenwood Press, Westport, Connecticut, 1975.

Lasson, Frans, and Svendsen, Clara. *Karen Blixen—En digterskœbne i billeder*. Gyldendal, Copenhagen, 1969.

Selborn, Clara. *Notater om Karen Blixen*. Gyldendals Paperbacks, Copenhagen, 1988.

Index